R.H.Joh

Sharks
of tropical
and temperate
seas

LES·ÉDITIONS·DU·PACIFIQUE

contents

foreword

This book is both a general review and field guide to the identification of species. It is designed to be of value to anyone having an interest in sharks, be it casual or scientific. Part I deals with sharks in general, primarily as they relate to man. In this regard, although Polynesia receives particular emphasis, sharks are discussed on a global basis with pertinent references to species occurring in various parts of the world. Included in this section is the best advice which can be given to date to those who find themselves in confrontation with sharks. Part II is devoted to systematics or the identification of species. This section has a key to the families of sharks, including the species known or thought to occur in Polynesia, here considered to approximate the triangle formed by the Cook, French Polynesian, and Hawaiian Islands. This key, which includes many species widely distributed in other tropical and temperate seas of the world, is followed by a detailed discussion of sharks occurring in the region of French Polynesia proper. This latter section, with few exceptions, includes only those species which have

been actually caught and positively identified.

Although the text of this book is intended to be self-explanatory, clarification of some additional points of format will aid the reader. Rather than burden the text with citations, small "exponent-like" numbers are used to identify source and reference material listed under *Literature Cited.* Both general writings and specific papers are included to provide the interested reader greater diversity. Regarding unit of measure conversions, i.e., English to metric, the accuracy of equivalents is in keeping with the context. Throughout the text species are referred to by common names, followed by the scientific name only after first mention of the species. The English common names used are: (1) those recommended by the American Fisheries Society[4], (2) those in wide use throughout the world and/or (3) those which, in the author's opinion, tend to reduce confusion. In part II the species discussed in detail are listed alphabetically within their respective families. Each species is introduced by its scientific name—including the date and author describing the species, the Tahitian and the English common names.

P: 2   Reef whitetip shark.   Below: blackfin reef shark.

PART I

defiled savages
of the sea

Since primordial times, sharks have reigned as dominant predators among the myriad life forms in the sea. Paradoxically, man, with his reasoning mind, has often failed to understand this role. Early in this century the opinion of many was that sharks were scavengers and cowards, and it was seriously questioned whether or not they did, in fact, attack man[74]. The resulting controversy sparked an accumulation of information which eventually left no doubt that man does on occasion fall victim to sharks. This theme, sensationalized in recent writings and films of fiction, has resulted in the present irrational fear and inaccurate understanding of these predators. The judgement of many is so affected that they can no longer enter the sea without fear of sharks—let alone consider their possible benefit or think of them as the magnificent animals of power, beauty and grace which in fact they are. The pendulum has gone full swing and sharks, once viewed as scavengers and cowards, are now thought of as savage killers—a reputation which cannot be supported by the facts.

Among the oceans predators, sharks are less savage in their dealing of death than killer whales, less ferocious than the sea crocodile, and yet they alone are the epitome of what man fears in the sea. This, when not more than 100 persons per year throughout the world are attacked by sharks and fewer than 50% of these attacks are fatal. In comparison, 300 persons per year die in the U.S. alone from such seemingly unlikely causes as bee stings or lightning. Surely, even a glance at these meager facts immediately indicates sharks are hardly savage killers. If, indeed, they were savage killers or man eaters, few people could enter the sea and return unharmed, for sharks possess such acute senses, have such wide distribution and occur in such large numbers, that few persons could enter the sea undetected. In reality, most persons entering the sea, be they bathers, swimmers, or divers, have unknowingly encountered sharks, which were inadvertently frightened away or not interested. The facts indicate it is only the rare or extenuating circumstance which results in sharks attacking man.

A rational understanding of sharks is hindered perhaps most by the abundance of popularly held misconceptions about these predators of the sea. A classic example is the widely held belief that sharks are unpredictable. In actuality each passing year provides added evidence that sharks do possess a degree of predictability, at least equaling that of other animals, and the heretofore unpredictable nature of sharks is almost assuredly the result of man's ignorance of their behavior. A point has now been reached where behavioral countermeasures, based upon the predictable aspects of shark behavior, can be employed by man to avoid injury in the vast majority of encounters. This subject will be dealt with later in detail.

Another problem hindering a proper understanding of sharks lies in the fact that people tend to think of them as fish of essentially the same nature, i.e., lending themselves to generalizations. In fact, quite the opposite is true. Sharks are a relatively diverse group of fishes placed together on the basis of rather general anatomical and morphological similarities. Their natural histories are otherwise as varied as the number of species which make up the group. Therefore, generalizations are, at best, most appropriate for select groups of sharks or those which have in common certain specific aspects.

With these limitations in mind, it is hoped the information which follows will help develop a more realistic understanding of sharks. This new understanding should place the shark hazard in proper perspective and permit sharks to be viewed as a natural resource to be utilized for man's benefit, while simultaneously allowing the shark to fulfill its role which nature has ordained.

the divine predators

Since time immemorial, the shark has occupied a prominent place in the minds of men. Its image is found among ancient drawings, e.g., those of Australian aborigines, and among ancient seafaring people it has been worshiped as a god. Even modern man regards the shark with a special awe and fascination instilled by few other animals.

Gods of Hawaii[74]

Among Polynesians, the Hawaiians seem to have had the most elaborate beliefs in the special powers of the shark. During ocean passages, they would call upon it in times of need to direct them towards land, produce favorable winds and otherwise assist them in their travels. These ancient ocean voyagers even equipped their canoes with offerings for the shark gods, the juice of the "awa", a native fish, being considered the most effective in soliciting aid. At Pearl Harbor, Oahu, an ancient arena existed where gladiators, armed with weapons fashioned of sharks' teeth, fought against large sharks. These combats are thought to have had a religious significance. Each of the islands of Hawaii had its own shark god, possessed of lesser power than the king of all Hawaiian sharks, *Kamo-hoa-lii,* who reputedly lived off Honolulu harbor. Many legends of *Kamo-hoa-lii* and the lesser shark gods have survived, most of them attributing phenomenal powers to these creatures, ranging from the ability to assume a human form, to that of controlling the elements. Although possessed of the ability to do good, these Hawaiian shark gods were feared, and few men ever endeavored to face or seek them out. In Hawaii these legends are generally viewed as merely interesting tales from another time, and only a few persons still living today place any faith in them.

Tahitian deities[70]

Among many of the islands of French Polynesia, the deification of the shark still remains a very real part of daily life. Basically, it is believed that ancestors are manifest in

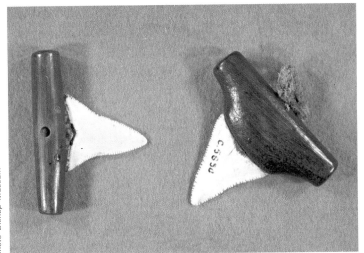

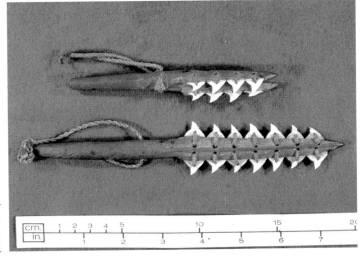

Throughout much of the Pacific, shark teeth—one of nature's finest cutting instruments—were fashioned by ancient people into various impliments for tools and weapons. **Upper**: *An impliment of the type used by ancient Hawaiians to kill large sharks during gladiatorial contests.*

the form of a shark called *Taputapua,* usually a very large one, which can be called upon by members of the family for assistance. In the case of domestic disagreements *Taputapua* can be called on to avenge one's honor, which is the reason for the widespread reluctance of spearfishermen to work at sea after fights with their wives. *Taputapua* can also be called upon for other feats, such as transporting a person upon its back from one island to the next. These are not just stories of the past ; persons still living today claim to have witnessed such events. A number of persons at Rangiroa Atoll adamantly believe their families have a *Taputapua.* One villager related having witnessed, as a child, a member of his family depart with their *Taputapua* to arrive safely at another atoll. Because of this belief, some local people do not want to have sharks fished or disturbed. Another person at Rangiroa said that in ancient times an image in the form of a shark was anointed daily by the families who communicated through it with their *Taputapua* in the sea. This same villager says that such an image existed not long ago somewhere in the Gambier island group.

the benevolent benefactors

It has been stated that everything about a shark is of use except for the snap of its jaws and the lash of its tail, but as astutely pointed out by a colleague, Hollywood has even capitalized on this aspect, featuring sharks in full length films. Although the shark can be used by man in its entirety, it is only sporadically exploited, and stable fisheries exist in only a few parts of the world.

Family jewels

One of the flourishing utilizations of sharks is the frivolous and fanciful use of teeth in the making of jewelry. In Tahiti the tooth of the tiger shark, *Galeocerdo cuvier,* brings the highest price, with an average jaw selling for over 15,000 cfp ($ 200.00 U.S.). One exceptional specimen (for museum

Jewler displaying gold mounted tiger shark tooth pendants.

exhibition) reputedly sold for 120.000 cfp ($ 1,500.00 U.S.). In New Zealand, it is the mako, *Isurus oxyrinchus,* tooth that is held in highest esteem.

Fishing for fun[44]

Certain sharks are fished for sport in various parts of the world. New Zealand anglers seek the mako, and have caught one of 3.66 m (12 ft.) and 455 kg. (1,000 lbs.). The Australians pride themselves in the catch of the largest fish to be landed on rod and reel. This record catch was a white shark, *Carcharodon carcharias,* 1,211 kg. (2,664 lbs.). Britons annually catch several thousand porbeagle, *Lamna nasus,* purely for sport, although this lively shark is also edible and of commercial value. In French Polynesia the mako and even the oceanic whitetip shark, *Carcharhinus longimanus* occasionally take trolled baits, providing sportfisherman with an unexpected catch[33].

Food, fins and fertilizer

Perhaps the most practical aspect of the shark is its nutritive value. In the past only about 1 % of the world's fish catch, consisted of shark[25], mainly because it has not been a popular food fish. In many parts of the world the thought of eating shark is repulsive. To these people it would no doubt come as a surprise to know that the fish in "fish and chips" in England and Australia often consists of shark[25,44]. In England, it is the spiny dogfish, *Squalus acanthias,* which is used, while in Australia it is the school shark, *Galeorhinus australis.* Japan also has an extensive shark fishery which uses the flesh of shark for food, and over 25 shark dishes are currently served in Japanese households[25]. In Hawaii, investigators tested the palatability of the sandbar shark, *Carcharhinus plumbeus,* and found it of good quality[67]. The leopard shark, *Triakis semifasciata,* the blue shark, *Prionace glauca,* the blackfin reef shark, *C. melanopterus,* and the mako shark are a few of proven palatability[33]. Ciguatera fish poisoning is unknown in shark—except in its liver[2]—and its flesh is, in this respect, well suited to the production of bulk protein. In remote areas, shark meat can be salted and dried in order to preserve it before shipping to other markets. This economical technique could be of special value in underdeveloped countries lacking the facilities for fresh transport and in need of basic protein resources. Mexico has, in fact, been doing this successfully for some time[25]. The Chinese even use the fins of sharks to make excellent soup. All the fins except the upper lobe of the tail fin and the pelvic and anal fins of small specimens, are of value. They are dried and later, through a cooking process, the supporting fin structures or ceratotrichia are extracted for use in the making of this unique soup. Shark's remains can be reduced for utilization as fertilizer, or converted to fish meal by the addition of cereal products, making excellent animal fodder (70% protein and 15% nitrogen)[74].

Leather and oil[74]

Shark hide, although requiring special attention because of its characteristic abrasive placoid scales which must be removed, produces a leather equal or superior to any in existence, having 2 or 3 times the tensile strength of pig or cow hide. Unfortunately, few tanneries are still operating, primarily due to an inadequate supply of hides. Should shark fisheries for food be developed, the leather industry would no doubt arise anew and flourish, as it once did when sharks were fished for oil from which Vitamins A and E were extracted. Although shark oil was of value in other uses, e.g., steel tempering, tanning, as a base for paints, and in manufacturing where oil of low specific gravity was desired, the synthetization of vitamins A after World War II resulted in the collapse of this industry. Shark oil was also reputed to be of medicinal value in the treatment of certain diseases, e.g., whooping cough, tuberculosis and rheumatism.

Guinea pigs of the sea

Sharks are beneficial to man in a rather unexpected way. They are ideally suited for numerous physiological studies and are now commonly used as laboratory animals. Sharks can withstand many times the radioactivity that most animals can tolerate, and they are virtually without cancer and many other diseases. This has prompted investigations into the reasons why. They are also being used in numerous other investigations, including the study of kidney function, osmoregulation, metabolism, immunoglobulin and antibody formation, to mention but a few[25].

nature's splendid creations

Of the approximately 21,000 species of fish identified, only about 250 or so are sharks. They are found in all oceans of the world, except the Antarctic[26], usually at less than 1,000 m (over 3,000 ft) although some sharks occur much deeper. Most of them, however, inhabit temperate or sub-tropical seas and some even enter fresh water and live in lakes. The tiniest of the lot is *Squaliolus laticaudus,* about 15 cm (6 in.) long, at maturity, while the leviathian, the whale shark, *Rhincodon typus,* is the largest fish on earth, attaining a length of 18 m (59 ft) and a weight of 41,000 kg. (90,000 lbs)[47].

In antiquity

Sharks existed in the primordial seas of the Devonian geological period nearly 350,000,000 years ago[29], a long time compared to man's most liberally estimated date of emergence just 5,000,000 years ago. Although sharks and their relatives were once considered the second most primitive among the living vertebrate classes (see opposite), they are now recognized as more modern than bony fish. Bony fish date back even earlier than sharks[29 43], and cartilage, a structural characteristic of sharks, once considered the evolutionary predecessor of bone, is now considered degenerate and represents a more modern specialization[29]. Moreover, the reproductive system of sharks is the near equal of mammalian forms, which is the most advanced procreational mechanism[61]. In spite of this newly recognized status in the evolutionary scale, sharks and their relatives remain among the most unchanged of the vertebrate classes. So successful has been their adaptation that some modern genera and species existed 180,000,000 years ago, dating

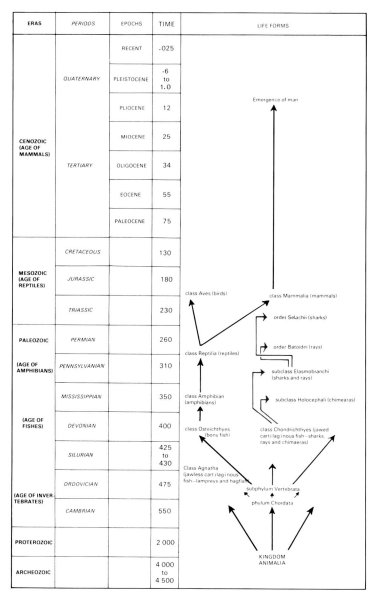

ERAS	PERIODS	EPOCHS	TIME	LIFE FORMS
CENOZOIC (AGE OF MAMMALS)	QUATERNARY	RECENT	.025	
		PLEISTOCENE	·6 to 1.0	
		PLIOCENE	12	
	TERTIARY	MIOCENE	25	
		OLIGOCENE	34	
		EOCENE	55	
		PALEOCENE	75	
MESOZOIC (AGE OF REPTILES)	CRETACEOUS		130	
	JURASSIC		180	
	TRIASSIC		230	
PALEOZOIC (AGE OF AMPHIBIANS) (AGE OF FISHES) (AGE OF INVERTEBRATES)	PERMIAN		260	
	PENNSYLVANIAN		310	
	MISSISSIPPIAN		350	
	DEVONIAN		400	
	SILURIAN		425 to 430	
	ORDOVICIAN		475	
	CAMBRIAN		550	
PROTEROZOIC			2 000	
ARCHEOZOIC			4 000 to 4 500	

Phylogenetic diagram of vertebrate classes showing their evolutionary relationship over the geological history of the earth (time in millions of years to beginning of interval). Red lines indicate group origin not related to geologic time scale.

extant forms further back into antiquity than any other vertebrate group[62]. Their success, however, has not been universal as certain species have not survived the test of time. Perhaps the most notable of the species to have succumbed was *Carcharodon megalodon,* very similar to the present day white shark. The principal difference between the extant and extinct white shark is size, for *C. megalodon,* probably the largest fish to have ever lived, is thought to have reached between 15[59] and 25 m[11 47] (50-80 ft) and some had 20 cm (8 in.) teeth[11]. This species was decidedly predaceous, feeding on, among other things, baby cetothere whales (now also extinct), during the miocene geological period, some 15 to 25 million years ago.

Structure and related function

Although sharks now perhaps represent the third most primitive of the 7 vertebrate classes, they are still the most readily available generalized primitive vertebrate, which accounts for their use as the standard in teaching basic courses in anatomy and morphology. It is of value here to review some of this structure and its related function, which will assist in understanding the shark and its role in the natural environment.

Reproduction: In sharks reproduction is similar to man in that fertilization is internal. This requires a degree of cooperation on behalf of the mating individuals. The male generally grasps the female in the region of the pectoral fins with his jaws, resulting in minor wounds, while acquiring a position suitable for insertion of one of the paired intromittant organs, called claspers, into the cloaca of the female[14 44]. Claspers are modifications of the pelvic fins, consisting of a rolling or folding of the fin elongation. Upon erection the clasper is swung forward across the body medially, not laterally. Normally only one clasper is inserted during copulation. Once inserted, there is a rotation of the cartilage which results in a spur or claw penetrating the cloacal wall, anchoring the male intromittant organ in the female[27]; hence, the name "clasper". The siphon sac, associated with the male reproductive system, is filled with sea water prior to copulation, and when released, seminal fluid

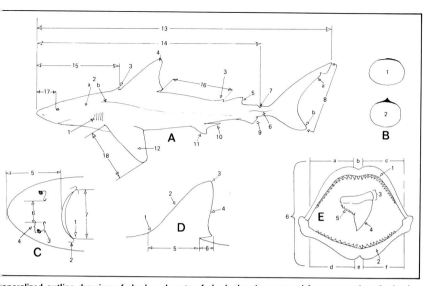

eneralized outline drawing of shark and parts of shark showing external features and methods of **easurement.**

A. *Lateral profile of shark.*

1. Gill slits.
2. Acustico-lateralis system.
a. Region of inner ear
b. Initiation of lateral line.
3. Dorsal fin spines.
4. First dorsal fin.
5. Second dorsal fin.

6. Caudal keel.
7. Precaudal pit.
8. Caudal or tail fin.
a. Upper lobe.
b. Lower lobe.
9. Anal fin.
10. Clasper, male organ.
11. Pelvic fin.

12. Pectoral fin.
13. Total length (tl).
14. Precaudal length (pcl).
15. Snout to first dorsal fin lg
16. Interdorsal dist.
17. Snout to eye lg.
18. Pectoral fin lg.

B. *Cross section of shark's body between dorsal fins.*

1. Without interdorsal ridge.
2. With interdorsal ridge.

C. *Underside of head.*

1. Inner labial groove.
2. Outer labial groove.

3. Nasal flap.
4. Nostril or naris (nares-plural).

5. Snout length.
6. Internasal dis.
7. Mouth width.

D. *Dorsal fin.*

1. Origin
2. Front margin.

3. Apex.
4. Rear margin.

5. Base distance.
6. Free rear tip.

E. *Features of jaw and teeth.*

1. Upper jaw.
2. Lower jaw.

3. Base of tooth.
4. Cusp of tooth.

5. Tooth serrations.
6. Dental formula:

(expressed as N° of teeth in region a-c of jaw, over region d-f) or

$$\frac{a = N° \text{ teeth upper right, } b = N° \text{ center upper teeth, } c = N° \text{ teeth upper left}}{d = N° \text{ teeth lower right, } e = N° \text{ center lower teeth, } f = N° \text{ teeth lower left}}$$

and sperm are washed along the crevice of the clasper into the cloaca of the female. Although a leaky system, it is obviously effective in obtaining the desired results.

With the exception of the basking shark *Cetorhinus maximus,* which produces thousands of tiny eggs and perhaps the Greenland shark, *Somniosus microcephalus,* all other sharks produce large, yolky eggs[44]. The development of these eggs follow three basic patterns[44]: *A) Oviparous.* This mechanism exists in primitive sharks, mostly bottom dwelling types, such as the horn sharks (family Heterodontidae), the cat sharks (family Scyliorhynidae), and also the whale shark (family Rhincodontidae). The eggs are encased in a leathery shell and expelled into the sea where the embryos develop for a period of 6 to 10 months—hatching as miniature adults. These eggs vary in size from a little over 3 cm long (just over 1 in.) in the dwarf shark *Galeus piperatus,* to over 35 cm (14 in.) in the whale shark. *B) Ovoviviparous.* This mechanism occurs in the majority of sharks, including the sand sharks (family Odontaspidae), the thresher sharks (family Alopiidae), the mako, porbeagle and probably the white shark (family Lamnidae), the tiger shark and a few others (family Carcharhinidae). The eggs develop from the nutrition of the yolk, and the embryos hatch in the mother, to be born shortly afterwards. The gestation period lasts about 9 months; an exception is the spiny dogfish, *Squalus acanthias,* which has a gestation period of two whole years[44]. *C) Viviparous:* This is the most sophisticated mechanism of development. It occurs in a number of sharks, including the smooth dogfish (family Triakidae), the blue shark, the oceanic whitetip, and others (family Carcharhinidae), and probably all of the hammerheads (family Sphyrnidae). The embryo develops internally obtaining nutrition, in addition to that provided by the yolk, via an umbilical cord from the mother. The normal gestation period lasts nine months.

Although a few sharks produce litters of nearly 100 pups, litters of 5 to 15 are more common. In the sand shark, *Odontaspus taurus,* only two pups are born due to a unique developmental mechanism; 15 to 20 eggs enter each of the

---

Upper: *Male reef whitetip shark with one clasper (sexual intromittant organ) erected.* **Middle**: *Female gray reef shark with mating scars.* **Bottom**: *A tiger shark embryo.*

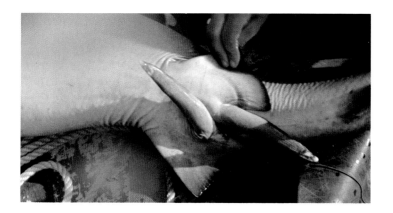

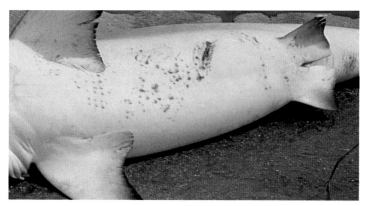

two oviducts, but only one in each oviduct produces an embryo. These embryos feed upon the remaining eggs, and the twins continue their development as the female produces more eggs to support their appetites. This system of development, "intrauterine cannibalism", also occurs in the porbeagle and possibly a few other species[44].

Respiration: Sharks are somewhat erroneously considered destined to a life without rest, because some need to swim continuously in order to move water past the gills to oxygenate the blood. Nevertheless, a substantial number of species are quite capable of resting on the bottom in still water, while muscularly pumping water over the gills. This ability is complete in bottom dwelling species, but it is also common to a lesser extent among others, including some of the largest sharks, e.g., the tiger shark[39]. Even among the more active sharks once considered incapable of breathing without incessant forward motion, exceptions are continually being discovered. For example, the bull shark, *Carcharhinus leucas,* has been found at rest on the sand after being hooked[13]; the gray reef shark, *C. amblyrhynchos,* has been observed motionless in aquaria[46] as well as in the sea[37 64]; and Springer's reef shark, *C. springeri,* has been discovered in repose in underwater caves in Mexico[13]. For all but the bottom dwelling sharks, however, it is true that relentless swimming is the rule, for much energy is required of most sharks to pump water past the gills because of their poorly developed branchial musculature.

Locomotion: Large or small, all sharks possess an asymmetrical tail fin with the upper lobe more or less elongated. As the shark performs its sinuous movement in the sea, this heterocercal tail fin, as it is called, creates a greater forward force at the top resulting in a downward element of thrust. The latter acts against the planing undersurfaces of the shark, specially the pectoral fins, which provide lift—much as the wings of an aircraft. In this fashion, although there are frictional losses, the forward force is balanced to provide proper propulsion[7]. This mechanism appears to be an adaptation which, in sharks living near the bottom, serves to pro-

The shark's unique asymetrical (heterocercal) tail in combination with the planing undersurfaces, especially the wing-like pectoral fins, provides efficient propulsion. Gray reef shark pictured.

vide propulsion without the lower lobe interfering with the substrate. Some pelagic sharks, needing speed more than maneuverability near the bottom, have more nearly symmetrical heterocercal tails providing greater thrust.

Some authors consider sharks generally slow, but from one species to the next swimming ability and speed varies immensely. Some of the bottom-dwelling sharks are barely capable of evading a diver, while more typical species are capable of considerable bursts of speed. The stomach contents of certain species, e.g., the pelagic mako and the white shark, indicate that they are capable of out-swimming some of the sea's fastest creatures including the porpoise, the sea lion and even the swordfish[44]. There is an explanation for this impressive ability in these sharks. The exertion of muscular energy creates heat, and in these species a circulatory mechanism has evolved, whereby the blood, warmed by muscular action, transfers its heat to the incoming cold blood. This heat-exchange mechanism warms the tissue, which physiologically provides for greater energy output per unit muscle, and this accounts for the speed and power of these particular sharks. However, although having warm blood, i.e., at a temperature in excess of the surrounding water, as it is not maintained at a constant level but fluctuates in accordance with environmental change, these sharks are not truly warm-blooded.

Buoyancy: In the absence of forward motion, a shark will sink to the bottom. However, although lacking a gas or swim bladder, the liver, which weighs, less than the water it displaces due to the stored fats and oils, provides considerable buoyancy[5 7]. The liver, although serving other functions appears especially important as a buoyancy mechanism[5] and as such is not completely passive. Sharks which have been burdened by the addition of weight are found to compensate by increasing the amount of light fats and oils within the liver, thereby increasing its buoyancy accordingly. Moreover, as growth occurs, a shark's mass increases at a faster rate than does its surface area which provides lift. If this were unchecked, the shark would become increasingly heavier, with respect to the water displaced, making it more

Buoyancy provided by the liver permits a diver to swim this dead 674 lb (306 kg) tiger shark through the water without sinking.

difficult to stop itself from sinking. Again, however, the liver compensates for this change in buoyancy associated with growth. As a consequence, extremely large sharks have immense livers. An example is a white shark caught in the 1940's off Cuba, which measured 6.41 m (21 ft) and weighed 3,320 kg (7,302 lbs). The liver weighed 457 kg (1,005 lbs), about 1/7th the body weight. So effective is the liver as a buoyancy mechanism that some sharks hardly need to move to provide lift. Indeed, the gray nurse shark, *Odontaspis arenarius,* of Australia, can nearly hover over the bottom, and the white shark can essentially pivot around its snout, an impossible task for most sharks. There are other benefits in not having a gas-filled swim-bladder. Any fish having such a mechanism finds its buoyancy negative if it suddenly descends or positive if it suddenly ascends. This is due to the compression and expansion of the compressible gas within the swim-bladder being acted upon by the new pressure associated with the changed depth. Being possessed of buoyancy in the form of fats and oils stored in the liver— essentially incompressible liquids—sharks can rapidly change depth, even over extremes, without adverse effect. This explains why sharks, e.g., the spiny dogfish, can be hooked at a depth of 300 m (1,000 ft) and immediately be hauled to the surface to survive in aquaria[55].

Skin: The hide of a shark is extremely thick and tough, covered with countless tiny placoid scales which, because of their similarity to teeth, are often called denticles. These denticles are arranged so that the cusps point backwards. This gives sharks a smooth texture when brushed from head to tail, but brushed in any other direction, sideways or, especially, from tail to head, the hide in extremely abrasive. A thrashing shark will produce substantial wounds on human flesh which look and feel like rope burns.

So tough is the hide, it was reported that during the capture of a whale shark, a 12 gauge shotgun blast of N° 2 shot fired into the back at a distance of 60 cm (2 ft) bounced off the 10 cm (4 in) thick hide, leaving only a circular depression[44].

Jaws, dentition and their use: Most of the effectiveness of

Cutting teeth, sometimes found in both jaws, are typically found in just the upper jaw of most fish-eating (picivorous) sharks, e.g., the galapagos shark teeth pictured.

the shark's feeding apparatus lies in the cutting abilities of the teeth, which are hard enough to cut metal. Their powerful jaws are capable of applying 60 kg (132 lbs) across the surface of a single tooth in the average 2 m (6 1/2 ft) shark[26]. Combined with the momentum of a large shark, such an apparatus allows it to cut chain or stainless steel cable[33]. In order to facilitate this cutting ability, the upper jaw not being fused to the cartilaginous skull (chondocranium)[11] is protrusable. Accordingly sharks can obtain a hold in any position, contrary to the common misconception that they must roll over to bite. When biting, violent shaking of the head and wrenching of the trunk serves to sever or cut free a morsel.

The tooth of the shark is actually a modified placoid scale or denticle. Like the denticles which are attached to the skin tissue, the teeth are attached to the gums in several rows rather than imbedded in the jaw. As the gum tissue grows forward, moving over the edge of the jaw, mechanical tension erects the mature teeth. This results in a continual succession of teeth. The old ones, if not lost in the course of feeding activity, eventually fall out as a consequence of the forward progression of gum tissue. The rate of tooth replacement is quicker in young specimens, and varies from as little as 7 days to several months, depending on the species and maturity. Generally, there are only 1 or 2 functional rows of teeth in each jaw, although some species have several rows of functional teeth in one or both jaws.

The variations in shark tooth structure are almost innumerable, being as diverse as the species which make up the group. In the plankton feeding basking and whale sharks, the thousand or so tiny teeth are essentially vestigial. Their function has been replaced by gill rakers or spongy tissue that serve principally to provide sustenance by sifting minute organisms from the sea. Some sharks possess jaws and teeth which are modified for the crushing of invertebrates, but many species that do not possess specialized dentition also feed on such prey. The soft squid and octopus (cephalopods) are fair game for almost all sharks. Most of the active predators are

Holding teeth, typically found in the lower jaw of most fisheating sharks, are sometimes alike in both jaws, as is the case with the exaggerated mako shark teeth pictured.

basically fish eaters "piscivorous" and many extend their diet to turtles and sea mammals. These sharks possess the most common type of dentition which consists of more or less broadly triangular, blade-like teeth with sharp cutting edges in the upper jaw and narrowly triangular, spike-like teeth in the lower jaw. In this arrangement, the lower teeth, which are the first to penetrate, serve principally to hold the prey, while the upper teeth serve principally for cutting. There are, however, exceptions. The tiger shark, for example, has similar teeth in both the upper and lower jaws which serve simultaneously to hold and cut. In any case, a shark's tooth is unique to the species and, therefore, of value in identification—both on the basis of form and arrangement. (See page 17, E-6 for computation of the dental formula useful in shark identification.)

Frequency of feeding and metabolism: Considered by many to be voracious savages, sharks surprisingly enough feed less often than is commonly thought. Although sharks can and do on occasion make gluttons of themselves, in captivity where food is generally more available, adults normally feed only 2 or 3 times a week. Such sharks maintain good health while consuming as little as 3 to 14% of their body weight per week[44]. However, it is known that in the wild their growth is slower[71], probably due to the scarcity of food. This is in accord with the finding that under natural conditions typical sharks, e.g., the gray reef shark, feed only once every 6 to 12 days, generally on a single small fish of 30 cm (12 in) or less[71]. Bottom-dwelling sharks can often survive for weeks on a single feeding. It is speculated that basking sharks off Britain, after shedding their gill rakers used to strain plankton from the sea, may go the entire winter without feeding[44]. Gravid females of several species, including the sandbar shark and the bull shark, are known to refrain from eating during the latter period of pregnancy, and males sometimes cease feeding during the mating season. Under otherwise normal conditions, sharks endure fasting only out of necessity, during which times they may rely on the reserves of the liver to survive. Under conditions of starvation,

Specialized teeth particularly suited to the crushing and grinding of hard shelled invertebrates are generally alike in both jaws, e.g., the Indo-Pacific nurse shark teeth pictured.

some bottom-dwelling sharks, e.g., the California horn shark, *Heterodontus francisci,* and the swell shark, *Cephaloscyllium ventriosum,* have survived approximately 9 to 15 months without feeding[39], but the more active sharks, e.g., the gray reef shark and the blackfin reef shark, generally only survive about 6 weeks without eating[66].

The act of feeding, in terms of physics, is a frugal utilization of energy. The stomach contains acids strong enough to act upon metal. Beyond the stomach is another specialization, generally termed the spiral valve. This mechanism, although it takes several forms, provides increased surface area which effectively increases absorption; hence, sharks have a very short intestine. Energy thus obtained can be stored at least in part, in the liver. This efficient reduction and storage of consumed matter, combined with the sharks efficiency of movement, helps to account for their ability to survive on little food[7], and as a rule, the larger the shark, the lower the basal metabolism[44].

Sensory perception: The shark is equipped with a battery of senses so finely integrated that they produce one of the most successful predatory groups on earth. So diverse and intricate are these senses, that science has yet to unravel all their mysteries.

Audition: The term as used here is the distant perception of any vibrational stimuli, and in sharks it represents the longest range sensory system. Studies indicate that acoustic sensing in sharks is specialized to perceive hydrodynamic sounds, which are produced by the movement of an object in water, e.g., rapid accelerations resulting during active feeding or by a wounded, struggling fish. However, sharks also perceive other sounds occurring within this range. Such sounds are characteristically low in frequency, ranging from near 10 to 800 Hz, and they are typically pulsed rather than continuous[52 53]. Peaks of hearing for most sharks fall below 100 Hz. These sounds can be perceived for at least hundreds of meters (or yards); this accounts for the often rapid appearance of sharks during spearfishing activities. As sound is propagated in water it causes physical disturb-

---

Gray reef sharks attracted to artificially produced, pulsed, low-frequency sounds simulating those of a struggling fish—16 mm sequence from just after commencement to end of a 3 minute test.

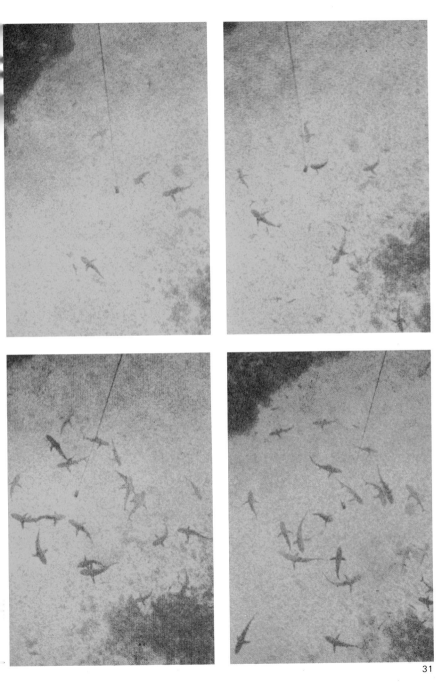

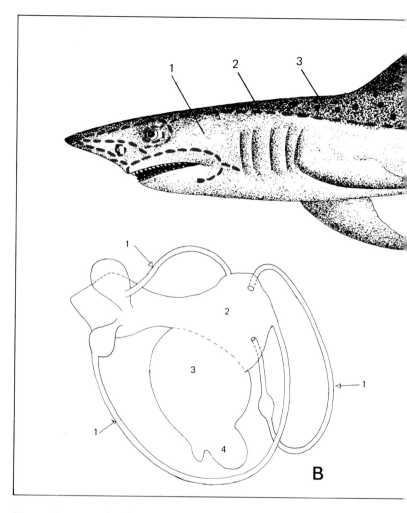

Diagramatic presentation of the sense organs used in hearing or the detection of mechanical disturbances in the water.

A. *External location of sense organs:*
1. Region of the inner ear.
2. Lateral line canal pores (dashed lines).
3. Pit organs (heavy red dots).

B. *Inner ear:* left side viewed as if the shark were cut longitudinally in the vertical plane. 1: semi-circular canals, 2: utriculus, 3: sacculus, and 4: lagena. Located within the sacculus and possibly the utriculus or lagena (situation unclear in sharks) are the principle receptors of hearing consisting of hair cells in contact with a dense otolith-like material. As a sound wave passes through the shark, the otolith-like

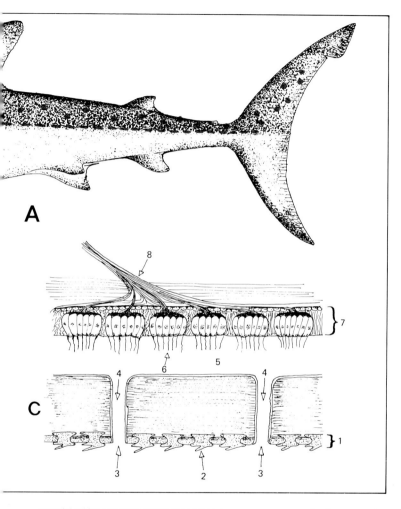

material which responds to the associated pressure wave more slowly, causes the hair cells to bend.

This triggers a nervous impulse mediating hearing.

C. *Lateral line canal:* left side viewed as if the shark were cut longitudinally in the horizontal plane. 1.: epidermis, 2: placoid scale or denticle, 3: external pore, 4: tubule, 5: canal, 6: neuromast sensory hair cells enclosed in a gelatinous cupulae, 7: neuromast and 8: nerve fibers. Along the lateral line canals are located neuromasts with sensory hair cells exposed to the internal canal fluid. As a disturbance impinges upon the shark, it is communicated to the internal canal fluid via external pores and tubules, which causes the hair cells to bend. This triggers a nervous response mediating perception.

ances, e.g., waves of pressure and particle motion, each of which vary according to the distance from a sound source. This phenomenon is the basis for the separation of underwater sounds into distant (far field) and close (near field) components, the more or less arbitrary dividing line in this continuum being defined as 1/5 a wave length for any given sound. The far acoustic field is predominated by pressure while in the near acoustic field, particle motion predominates. Sharks possess separate hearing mechanisms which are specifically adapted to perceive sounds characteristic of near and far fields. The inner ear being the most sensitive, is generally considered the far field acoustic receptor while the lateral line generally mediates near field sound perception, and both together are often referred to as the acoustico-lateralis system.

There exists no equivalent of the human outer and middle ear in sharks. The inner ear consists of paired organs (labyrinths) imbedded in the cartilaginous skull, just behind and above the eyes with no externally observable characteristics, except in some species for tiny endolymphatic pores on the top of the head. It consists of three tubular, semi-

circular canals and an enlarged, sac-like area divided into three distinct regions termed: utriculus, lagena and sacculus. Although the seat of hearing rests within the latter two structures in most fish, the situation may be different and is yet unresolved in sharks. Within these structures are sensory fibers in contact with a dense otolith-like material. As a propagated sound wave passes through the shark, the sensory fibers of different density are stimulated by shearing against this inertial-lagging dense body, mediating perception of far field sounds. As the utriculus mediates gravity perception (at least in most fish) and the semi-circular canals are essentially orientation receptors, only a portion of the inner ear mediates hearing.

The lateral line in sharks consists of a series of tubes or canals running parallel to and under the skin, several of which are in the head region and a major one each side running the length of the body. The latter is usually visible as a line along the trunk, hence the name. The tubes of the

The blue shark, very common in temperate but uncommon in tropical seas.

lateral line have openings or pores which communicate with the outside, and along the interior of the tubes are arranged sense organs, "neuromasts", with tiny gelatinous sensory fingers called cupulae[23]. As certain near field sounds reach the shark, the fluid within the lateral line system is set into motion causing the cupulae to bend. This produces a nervous impulse thereby mediating perception. In addition to this standard acoustic perception to near field sounds, it has been shown that fish, sharks included, have a distant touch perception. As the shark moves through the water, various disturbances—including a static bow wave—are created. This static bow wave is prominent in front of the snout and diminishes as it rounds the body towards the tail. When an object is encountered these disturbances are distorted, and this distortion is perceived via the lateral line and/or the free pit organs. The free pit organs are tiny depressions peppered over the shark's body. Within these depressions or pits are neuromasts, similar in structure to those of the lateral line canal. Once ascribed a taste function, these neuromasts are less sensitive than the lateral line neuromasts and are thought to serve direct as well as distant touch.

Olfaction: This term, as used here, pertains to the perception of water-born odors. Although acute in sharks, this sense is not as all—important as it was once thought to be. The shark, once considered a swimming nose, is now known to possess other equally important senses, and the olfactory lobes of the brain, once thought entirely devoted to perception of water-born odors, are now known to have other

---

An observation of potential pair formation and initial courtship in the blackfin reef shark, thought to be mediated via the sense of smell (olfaction). Like numbers indicate the respective positions of each shark at a given moment in time. Arrow indicates direction of current, carrying odor produced by bait. Solid line indicates path of lead shark (assumed female) which crossed perpendicular to the odor corridor, apparently uninterested in the bait. Dashed line indicates path of following shark (assumed male) which moments later was observed to swim up the odor corridor as if seeking the bait. At the point where the lead shark had crossed, the following shark made an abrupt right-angle turn. Up to and slightly beyond this point, visual contact between the two sharks was obstructed by the coral formation (positions 1 & 2)—indicating olfactory orientation. Moreover, the distance between these sharks closed rapidly, resulting in close-following behavior (positions 4 & 5) wherein the behavior of each changed, i.e., the lead shark swam an increasingly sinuous path in a tail-up manner while the following shark oriented to its vent. This was thought from other data[35] to represent initial courtship.

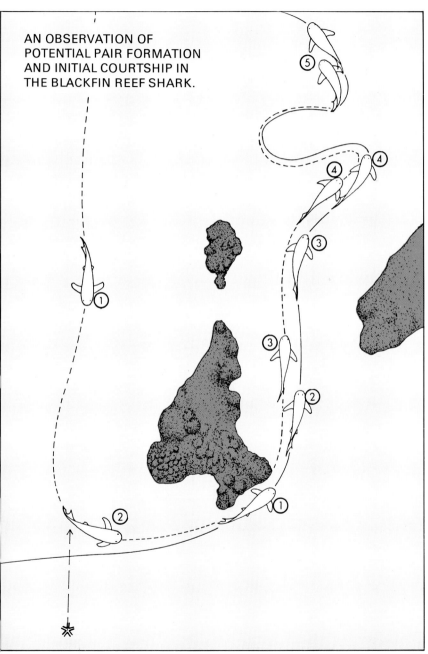

AN OBSERVATION OF
POTENTIAL PAIR FORMATION
AND INITIAL COURTSHIP IN
THE BLACKFIN REEF SHARK.

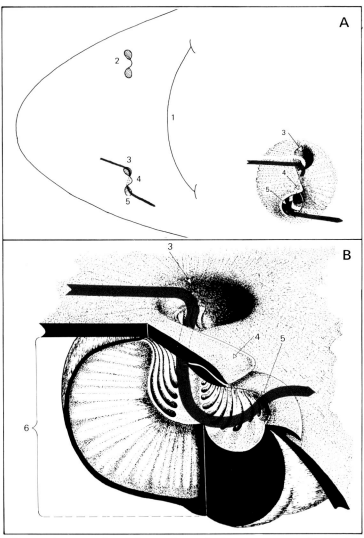

Diagramatic presentation of the nostril or naris—the sense organ used in the detection of water born odors. 1: mouth, 2: nostril or naris (nares: plural), 3: incurrent opening, 4: nasal flap, 5: excurrent opening, and 6: nasal sac (arrows indicate flow of water). **A.** Forward motion of the shark causes water to enter the incurrent opening of the nostril and pass through the nasal sac after which it departs the excurrent opening. **B.** Inside the nasal sac are folds of tissue which effectively increase the number of olfactory receptors exposed to the odor bearing water, thereby increasing sensitivity.

functions as well. Tests indicate that sharks perceive substances at least as dilute as 1 part per million[65]. In the sea they are routinely observed to follow odors for hundreds of meters (yards) and occasionally under optimal conditions, even kilometers (miles). Olfactory perception is obviously dependent upon the magnitude and continuity of the odor and its dispersal in the sea. Compared with auditory orientation, olfactory attraction has directional limitations and occurs at a slower rate after stimulus initiation.

At first thought one would view olfactory perception as only useful in detecting injured prey or when scavenging upon odiferous material. However, experiments have shown normal fish produce odors detected by sharks. Moreover, startled or alarmed fish produce a different odor which elicits food-seeking behavior in sharks[66]. Therefore, olfaction is potentially of value in normal predation of uninjured fish. There are also indications that sharks may use the sense of olfaction to perceive non-feeding related stimuli, e.g., sex identification or reproductive state[35]. This is in need of verification.

Water-born odors are perceived via the nasal pits or nares, paired organs found one on each side under the snout and forward of the mouth. These organs do not communicate with the mouth or buccal cavity as in man, but are dead ended and somewhat U shaped. They are formed in such a way as to permit water to enter one side and depart the other, providing a continuous flow over the olfactory receptors[23]. As an odor is approached, the shark generally swims to the side that has the strongest concentration as sensed by the respective naris, and if both nares are equally stimulated, it swims straight ahead to the source of the odor[56]. This directionality is enhanced in the course of normal swimming by the head moving from side to side, permitting the nares to sample a wider portion of the odor corridor. Currents affect orientation. Some species turn into the current upon detection of an attractant stimulus, and if the odor is lost, the shark will double back and pick up the odor once again to continue tracking it to the source.

Vision: Popularly conceived as poor of sight, sharks, in fact, possess a visual ability admirably adapted to their predatory habits. Their biggest failing appears to be in acuity, or the ability to discriminate fine detail, shape or form[68]. Although

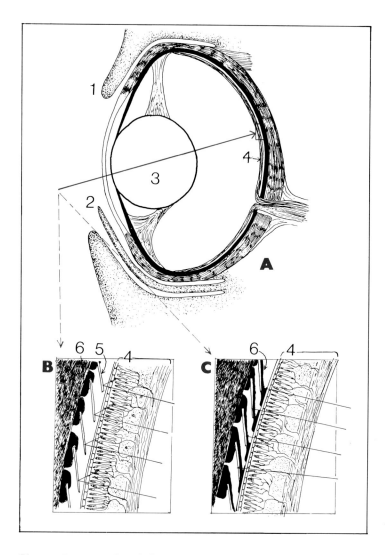

Diagramatic presentation of the eye illustrating mechanisms facilitating visual sensitivity.

1: immovable eyelid, 2: movable eyelid or nictitans, 3: lens, 4: retina, 5: tapetum lucidum, and 6: pigment cells (arrows indicate path of light). **A.** Light focused by the lens passes through the retina mediating vision in the normal manner. **B.** In sharks a unique mechanism, the tapetum lucidum, reflects the light back into the retina a second time, amplifying sensitivity. **C.** Certain sharks prevent over stimulation by occluding the tapetum lucidum via the migration of pigment cells.

gross form, e.g., the difference between horizontal and vertical rectangles, is easily recognized, discrimination between squares, circles and triangles becomes more difficult. It would appear that discrimination of more subtle forms is not possible. With regard to sensitivity or the ability to perceive objects and movement under low light levels, sharks have excellent vision[23][24]. This is due to unique, anatomical adaptations of the eye. Light enters the eye stimulating cells in the retina in normal fashion, but a reflective layer, the tapetum lucidum, reflects the light back through the retinal cells, thereby amplifying stimulation. Certain species possess an additional refinement; whereby, under normal levels of illumination, over-stimulation is prevented by the migration of pigment cells over the reflective tapetum lucidum. As darkness falls the occluded tapetum regains its full sensitivity, thereby providing the shark with a visual advantage over its prey. Although the eye of the shark is rich with rod cells mediating the above functions, certain species are known to possess cone cells probably mediating at least a limited degree of color vision. It is not known whether this color vision adds significantly to the sharks visual ability.

With such a visual apparatus, the shark is well equipped for its predatory ways. It senses both motion and contrast very well, which accounts for the often observed attraction of sharks to bright colors, e.g., in scientific literature "yum yum" yellow is described as particularly attractive[7]. It would appear that such attraction is based not on color but brightness or contrast difference, and anything which possesses such qualities is likely to catch the eye of the shark.

Electroreception: This is a sense only recently recognized which involves the perception of weak electrical fields. All muscular action produces electrical impulses; therefore, most life forms possess weak fluctuating electrical fields. Sharks, e.g., the dogfish, *Scyliorhinus canicula,* can detect such fields and have been stimulated into food seeking activity by the placing of electrodes under the sand[40]. In response to the electrical impulses emitted, the shark would bite the sand as if seeking flatfish or other concealed food. This indicates an obvious role in the natural environment.

As moving sea water (an electrical conductor) in the earth's magnetic field also has associated electrical gradients, it suggests a navigational mechanism whereby sharks could orient when out of sight of the bottom.

Electroreception is mediated via the ampullae of Lorenzini, which are aggregations of gelatinous filled tubes located on the top and bottom of the shark's head just forward of the eyes. This organ has previously been ascribed various functions, e.g., depth and temperature perception, but recent research indicates that it may serve principally for electroreception.

Gustation: The sense of taste in the shark is also operational, mediated via organs located in sensory pits within the mouth. Sharks have a definite discriminatory response regarding palatability, and although they often sample items, distasteful objects are quickly rejected.

Behavior

Activity, movement and migration: During recent investigation using conventional tagging (implantation of plastic spaghetti-like external markers) and telemetry tagging (electronic ultra-sonic emitters attached externally or fed internally), [37][54]several species of sharks have been shown to be quite localized and routine in their daily activity patterns. For example, among the gray reef shark, which commonly forms packs, an individual was found to remain during the day in a particular 0.5 km (0.3 mi) square area of an atoll lagoon, moving into the pass at sunset and spending the early evening hours at the pass entrance on the outer reef (see opposite). By midnight this shark would begin its return to the lagoon, spending a couple of hours in the center of the pass. The early morning hours were spent in very shallow water around a small island on the lagoon side of the pass. By sunrise, it moved back into its normal day time haunt in the lagoon. This pattern was repeated for 3 days—the life of the telemetry tag. The shark passed the same point in the pass, during its movements to the pass

---

Movements of a gray reef shark, for three consecutive days at Rangiroa Atoll.

Data obtained via telemetry tagging. Location established at 15 minute intervals, but where the shark remained at the same location during a given hour, its presence is indicated on the map by the hour (abbreviated) terminating the period, e.g., if the shark was found on location at 0815, 0830, 0845 and 0900, its presence for the given location on the map is indicated by the number 9: (0900 = 9).

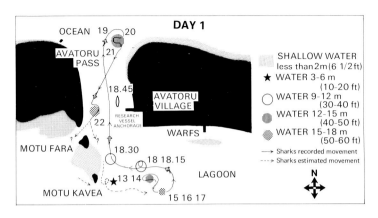

DAY 1

OCEAN 19 20

AVATORU PASS 21

18.45

AVATORU VILLAGE

RESEARCH VESSEL ANCHORAGE

22

WARFS

MOTU FARA 18.30

18 18.15

LAGOON

13 14

MOTU KAVEA 15 16 17

SHALLOW WATER less than 2m (6 1/2 ft)
★ WATER 3-6 m (10-20 ft)
◯ WATER 9-12 m (30-40 ft)
▥ WATER 12-15 m (40-50 ft)
▦ WATER 15-18 m (50-60 ft)
→ Sharks recorded movement
--→ Sharks estimated movement

N

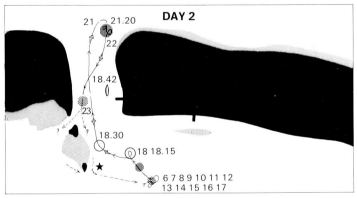

DAY 2

21 21.20

22

18.42

23

18.30

18 18.15

6 7 8 9 10 11 12
13 14 15 16 17

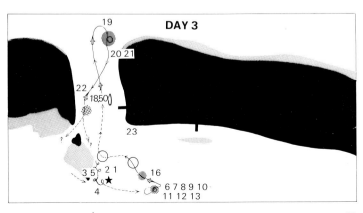

DAY 3

19

20 21

22

1850

23

3 5 2 1 16

4

6 7 8 9 10
11 12 13

entrance, within 10 minutes of the same time each day. Such a pattern, including an analysis of the fine movements, was indicative of nocturnal activity and feeding behavior. Similar routine, but different movements of the same general type, was noted in other individuals of this species[37]. In other species, e.g., the blackfin reef shark, the reef whitetip shark, *Triaenodon obesus*[54], and the blacktip shark, *Carcharhinus limbatus,* similar regularity of localized movements was noted. It was established that each species possessed its own characteristic type of movement, which varied in each individual. These movements were again basically nocturnal, and all species exhibited a degree of tidal periodicity, i.e., becoming active or moving into shallow water during slack tides (when there is no tidal current in the atoll passes) and especially during the low slack when the water was dirty. Conventional tagging showed that these species were basically resident. Some individuals remained in the same area for over three years (the period of observation). In the case of the gray reef shark, such residency in a given area was also accompanied by long association with the same individuals or pack members[37].

It would, therefore, appear that the movements of many sharks, particularly inshore species, are much more precise and predictable than has previously been thought. This, however, may not be true of all sharks, as some are possibly nomadic. The blue shark in California has been shown to possess both routine localized and perhaps nomadic long term movements. During a telemetry study, individuals were found to remain at sea during the day, while closely approaching land at night to feed on concentrations of spawning squid[63]. However, conventional tagging resulted in individuals being captured in one to three years' time up to 2,666 km (1,600 mi) away, off the coast of Mexico and Central America[25][51]. If, and when, these sharks would have ever returned to California waters is not known.

Seasonal movements or migrations are known in many species of sharks. On the Eastern Coast of the U.S., some 20 species are considered migratory, several of which move regularly up and down the coast over a distance of 1,333 km (800 mi) and others from inshore to offshore and back again[14][44][74]. In the Tuamotus, there is an indication that

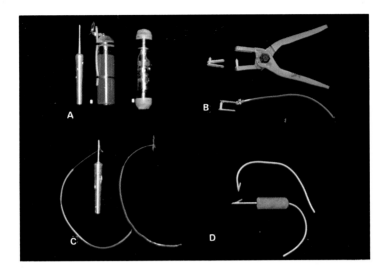

Upper A. *telemetry tags for external* **left** *and internal* **right** *application, and conventional:* B. *Roto fin crimp,* C. *Floy stainless steel (speargun applied), and* D. *Floy plastic dart tags. Color coded trailers* B & C *are investigator modifications to aid field identification.* **Lower**: *Atraumatic telemetry implantation is effected by placing a unit in a gutted fish which is fed to a shark.*

the gray reef shark may possess limited migratory movements or that it aggregates seasonally in certain areas to disperse after a time[37].

Feeding behavior: Sharks are among the few large predators that possess the ability to readily remove bite-size pieces from prey. In spite of this ability, most sharks commonly feed upon prey which can be swallowed whole. As a consequence, normal prey are usually related to the size of the shark. The white shark, which commonly reaches 5 to 6 m (20 ft) in length, not infrequently feeds on whole seals or porpoises, although it sometimes halves them[44]; while the gray reef shark, which generally does not exceed 2 m (6 1/2 ft), feeds commonly on fish usually under 30 cm (1 ft)[71].

Although sharks rely for their livelihood primarily on their ability as active predators, they are also fortuitous feeders, eating whenever the occasion arises. This feeding behavior varies from taking advantage of injured animals to scavenging on both edible and inedible items. In these endeavors, sharks may be stimulated to feed at times other than those usually reserved for normal predation, which for most species is during the hours of darkness. This accounts for the seldom reported observation of natural predation. Such predation has, however, been observed where the shark selected one fish and simply pursued it until captured in a cat-and-mouse-like fashion. Some sharks have been observed racing indiscriminantly through dense schools of fish, but as these were surface observations, it is not known to what degree they were directing pursuit toward an individual fish.

Under novel feeding situations, all sharks are much more cautious about their prey than is generally recognized. In this respect, however, there is a basic difference in behavior between inshore and pelagic or oceanic sharks. Inshore sharks are generally timid, and typically they are more reluctant to approach a diver. Pelagic sharks on the other hand, are often considerably more brazen, sometimes even brushing against or bumping into divers. But nearly all sharks generally exhibit a certain reluctance, especially in novel situations. This is usually expressed by the shark circling time and again, departing occasionally, only to return and resume its circling while moving closer. This is a type of instinctive

Upper: *A blackfin reef shark, more adept at feeding above the bottom, easily out-runs a reef whitetip shark in pursuit of a speared but escaped red snapper.* **Lower**: *A reef whitetip shark, one of the few carcharhinids adept at feeding among the coral, locates a speared fish placed on the sand which it quickly orients (head or tail first) in its mouth to be swallowed whole.*

evaluation or sizing-up of the prey, and only when the shark's apprehension is overcome by its desire to feed, will it move in to attack. Time, therefore, is an important factor where divers are concerned, as each passing minute brings the inquisitive shark closer to the realization that a diver represents relatively harmless and vulnerable prey. Of course, the shark is influenced by other factors. Experiments have shown that starved sharks are more responsive to feeding stimuli[66], and it seems logical to conclude that a hungry shark will take a greater risk in order to satiate its hunger.

Maturity seems important, for small sharks seem to lack respect for the hazards which might befall them, probably due to lack of experience. Immaturity and hunger in combination would seem responsible for the often noted greater aggressiveness of juveniles. These smaller individuals, not having been reduced in their number by predation and other environmental vicissitudes, have a higher population density. As a consequence of the resulting competition and increased metabolic requirements to support growth, juveniles appear to be in a state of greater hunger than adults. Even newborn sharks of any appreciable size should be respected. For example, a dusky shark, *Carcharhinus obscurus,* of about 1 m (3 ft), repeatedly attacked a diver biting him on the toes, fingers, arms and buttocks[58]. This shark was judged on the basis of size to be about 1 week of age. This is a particularly trying time in the life of a young shark, as nutrition received from the mother or the yolk sac up to this point becomes depleted, resulting in a famished little savage faced with the choice of eating or dying of starvation. Fortunately, such incidents are rare. Normally a diver is so disproportionately large that, in spite of the increased motivation, newborn and juvenile sharks are intimidated.

Social facilitation or the enhancement of the behavior of one individual, induced by the presence of others, is yet another factor which influences feeding situations. Where a feeding opportunity presents itself, several sharks may be attracted. Each essentially proceeds with its own instinctive process of sizing-up the prey, but the presence of the others, perhaps contributing a type of competitive pressure, acts as a

A few months old gray reef shark braves a bold bite just a yard (meter) in front of the cameraman.

catalyst. Attack may be some time in coming, depending upon the least reluctant individual to sufficiently overcome its apprehension. Under such circumstances, once the initial attack has started, the behavior of the remaining sharks, spurred on by the subsequent sight, sound and odor of first blood, is changed. All hesitation vanishes resulting in a holocaust which is generally termed a "feeding frenzy". Sharks frantically compete for a morsel. Their behavior, in the early stages, is often still directed towards the prey, but as some individuals become injured, they too may fall victim to the massacre. As the situation progresses, usually very rapidly, with blood and tissue blocking vision and further stimulating hungry sharks, anything becomes fair game. Boats can be attacked and overturned, and anything at all can become the object of mass feeding. Even such situations, however, have an end. If the source of food is essentially limitless, e.g., a whale carcass, the sharks will eventually satiate themselves, and feeding will gradually be reduced to a more individual endeavor. Eventually, relative calm will prevail, and the sharks will revert to their initial milling behavior. In cases where the food supply is quickly exhausted, relative calm is more quickly regained, but the remaining individuals are less satiated.

Social Behavior (behavior involving the interaction between individuals of the same or different species):

Aggressive behavior: Evidence indicates that sharks are aggressive in other than a feeding sense. Boats, seemingly a most unpalatable item, are not infrequently attacked, and the teeth sometimes remain in the hull as evidence[7]. Attack statistics, (over 1,500 case histories collected from all over the world by the American Institute of Biological Sciences under U.S. Office of Naval Research support), indicate many attacks on man—in fact the majority—appear to be motivated by other than the desire to feed[6][7][8]. During feeding-motivated attacks a shark would be expected to remove flesh from the victim and proceed to feed, perhaps even at an accelerated pace, as blood and tissue fluids saturate the area. Actually, only about 25% of attacks on

---

Only after numerous silky sharks were baited would a few of them become uninhibited enough to approach the bait offered by a diver.

record are of this nature[6]. Most cases consisted of a few quick attacks against the victim, which resulted in a slash type wound—where flesh was not removed—after which the shark departed. This type of behavior is not in keeping with what would be expected if feeding were the motivation. As these wounds resembled those found on sharks themselves, it was suggested that such attacks were socially motivated in a fighting sense[8]. Recent research has provided direct evidence confirming this speculation[34 36].

Moreover, certain species have been shown to enter a postural display prior to such attacks[34]. Of considerable significance is the fact that diver behavior, in certain incidents, was found to be responsible for eliciting display and subsequent non-feeding motivated attack. It was found that pursuit by divers, especially toward newly arriving sharks which had not become accustomed to the divers, and circumstances where cornering was involved, were the most effective in eliciting intense display. Other stimuli as well, e.g., pursuit by submersibles[45], unusual sounds[34], and quick movements[34], have been shown effective in eliciting display. Conversely, a strong feeding stimulus, e.g., the presence of speared fish where the shark is not denied access to the prey, appears to suppress display reducing the probability of non-feeding motivated attack[36].

Such display behavior is unmistakable in its intense form. It consists principally of an extraordinarily changed mode of swimming which is accompanied by a number of distinct postural or anatomical characteristics[34]. The shark swims in a fashion where extreme bending and twisting of the body occurs simultaneously with a laterally exaggerated swimming motion in which the head and tail almost touch on one side. In the course of providing forward motion this movement changes, so that the head and tail almost touch on the other side. This causes the head to pass through an arc which has been described by some observers as "head shaking" or more appropriately "head swinging". This description is somewhat misleading, as it is the contortion of the body and the exaggerated lateral swimming motion which gives basic character to the display. Some sharks vary this pattern slightly by adding a vertical component so that the movement results in a type of spiral gyration, while others tend to tilt

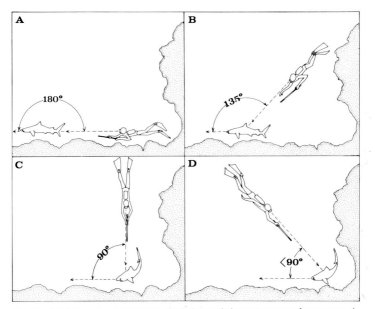

Relationship between escape route restriction and the occurrence of exaggerated-swimming display in the gray reef shark.
As recorded during test trials in which divers charged sharks. Displays were most intense or more easily illicited when escape route restriction was greatest.

Comparison between normal swimming and exaggerated-swimming display modes in the gray reef shark.
A. normal swimming: **B**. display, laterally exaggerated swimming and **C**. display, rolling (1-2-1) and spiral looping (1-6). Rolling, although similar to the initial phases of spiral looping, is distinct in that the shark returns to a level display attitude without entering into the up and down path seen in spiral looping.

Gray reef shark: **Top** *normal swimming behavior,* **Bottom** *typical mode of exaggerated-swimming display behavior characterized by: raised head and slightly open mouth, arched back, body bent laterally and dropped pectoral fins (see diag. top p. 56).*

Gray reef shark—alternate modes of exaggerated-swimming display behavior: **Upper** *rolling-exaggerated-swimming display and* **Lower** *spiraling-exaggerated-swimming display behavior (see diag. bottom p. 53).*

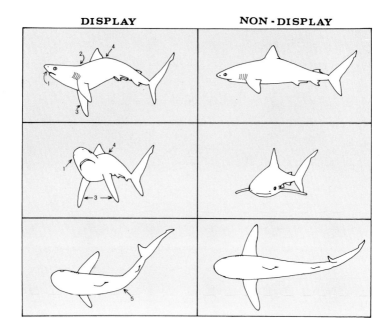

DISPLAY   **NON - DISPLAY**

Comparison between normal swimming and exaggerated-swimming display postural elements in the gray reef shark.

Arrows denote: 1) Lifting of the snout, 2) bend between chondocranium and spinal column caused by lifting of the snout, 3) pectoral fin depression, 4) arching of the back and 5) lateral bending of the body.

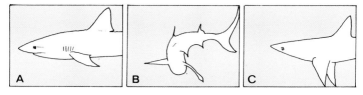

Comparison of pectoral fin positions in the gray reef shark.

During: **A**. normal swimming (relatively little pectoral fin depression), **B**. startle response (brief, moderate pectoral fin depression) and **C**. exaggerated-swimming display (prolonged, moderate to extreme pectoral fin depression).

the body axis. Although there are minor modifications, this behavior appears to be ritualized, i.e., essentially identical in its basic elements, in all individuals, indicating a behavior with long standing significance, probably of considerable value in other than man-shark encounters. Whatever the modification, "exaggerated-swimming display" is unmistakably different from the smooth graceful movements associated with normal swimming. Related to this display are distinctive anatomical changes: (1) the head is elevated, resulting in a slight opening of the jaws and an angle at the junction of the head and body, (2) the back is arched, (3) the body bends laterally, and (4) the pectoral fins become depressed, sometimes approaching a nearly vertical orientation.

It is not known with certainty what specific underlying motivation releases such exaggerated-swimming display behavior or related attacks. They are noted to occur under such a variety of circumstances, it seems no single motivations can adequately acount for all situations. However, it appears such display is a defensive behavior, serving to communicate threat, and that such communicative function may be elicited by any one of a number of underlying motivations related to social behavior, e.g., fright, anger, dominance or possibly territoriality. Display appears to occur where there exists conflict between positive and negative elements related to such social motivations, and subsequent attacks appear to be released by failure to behave in a fashion indicating recognition of this communicative function. These attacks are consequently unleashed in a fighting rather than feeding sense. Such attacks can be released without the forewarning of display, apparently by overt violation of one of the factors involved in the not yet clearly defined social code of sharks. Such attacks, whether preceded by display or not, unlike those motivated by feeding, are lightning fast and very brief— usually resulting in slash type wounds. Indeed, the author was involved in such an attack[36], where display was omitted, by a gray reef shark which had been hooked, tagged, transported and released during translocation experiments. The attack occurred after entering the water to observe the sharks condition during release. The specific motivation involved was difficult to pinpoint, but the shark responded as if angered, by the harsh treatment prior to release. Whatever the specific underlying motivation, the special circumstances involved indicated a non-feeding motivated type of attack. Display communicates threat which could conceivably be instrumental in facilitating several social behaviors including predator prey relationships, dominance and territoriality. (The latter two will be discussed seperately).

Regarding predator-prey relationships, display or non-feeding motivated attack may serve as an escape mechanism during encounters with potential predators. A strategic defensive attack by prey species can circumvent pursuit by potential predators. Moreover, flight is a universal releaser for attack, and display, as an alternative to fleeing, can serve to intimidate a predator and give time for gradual escape. The author has observed the gray reef shark in display oriented toward a large hammerhead on one occasion and another gray reef shark on another occasion[39]. The encounter with the hammerhead would be in keeping with such a mechanism. In this regard a very interesting experiment was performed by a graduate student in Miami[42]. He donned apparel resembling a killer whale, and simulating the swimming movements of this potential predator, he approached several confined lemon sharks. These sharks

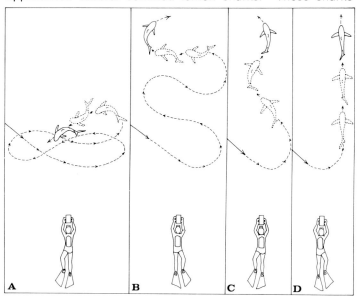

Comparison of swimming paths during normal swimming and various intensities of exaggerated-swimming display in the gray reef shark.
A. intense display, **B**. moderate display, **C**. mild display and **D**. normal swimming.

initiated a behavior similar to exaggerated-swimming display on such approaches but behaved normally during approaches by divers in customary apparel.

Although the above display behavior is only known to occur in two species, the gray reef shark and the galapagos shark, fragments of display and other similar postural movements have been observed in numerous other species[34], notably the hammerheads[48]. It appears that even in species where display is reduced or lacking, the same or related underlying motives may remain. This would account for the numerous non-feeding motivated attacks.

Dominance: Dominance is generally the preeminence of one individual or species over another, which biologically serves several functions, sometimes including intimidation of potential competitors from food. In certain sharks dominance exists both between individuals of the same species[34] (normally larger dominating smaller and even male dominating female) and between various species[34]. For example, it is reported that the silvertip shark is dominant over the galapagos shark while the blacktip is subordinate to both.

It would seem logical that exaggerated-swimming display could serve this end, and indeed a most convincing observation of such a mechanism at work was related

A gray reef shark takes the bait from out of the mouth of a blackfin reef shark—one of many incidents which can appear an expression of dominance but is in reality a case of "the best man (shark) wins".

recently by a reputable Rarotongan[72]. In this incident a moray eel was about to eat a recently speared but escaped fish. A gray reef shark appeared and was observed to direct a display posture towards the eel, which persisted in its efforts to feed on the fish. The shark abruptly terminated the display and attacked the eel, leaving a noticable white slash. The eel reportedly responded instantly by entwining itself around the sharks gill region. The shark dashed about rubbing the eel against the reef, finally dispelling it. Moreover, it is similarly reported[3] that during spearfishing, repeated denial of prey to a gray reef shark is sufficient to release display and subsequent attack. The above are but a few of the more obvious incidents of display possessing

A gray reef shark closely investigates the cameraman. Is this dominance, territoriality or curiosity? Probably the latter.

elements easily related to dominance. Many other incidents, perhaps the majority, can also, upon analysis, be reduced to elements related to dominance.

Territoriality: Certain sharks clearly possess a homerange (routinely frequented area), but territoriality (defense of exclusive access to a given area, e.g., fixed geographic, moving geographic or personal space) has not been adequately established. Only a few observations have been made which were advanced as indicating territoriality. In each case, the observed behavior did not strictly fit the definition and could be explained by other mechanism, e.g., dominance. Moreover, extensive observations of sharks and other sea creatures in close association, under both unstimulated and baited situations, do not support either geographic[9,36] or personal space[36] types of territoriality in the strict sense.

Certain observations, advanced as evidence indicating territoriality, have involved exaggerated-swimming display which was thought to indicate defense of a given area[8 45]. Again, these observations did not fit the definition in its strict sense as there was no indication that the particular shark defended its area from other sharks or fishes, and this behavior could be explained by other mechanisms, e.g., dominance—especially since dominance may be greatest for animals in surroundings which are most familiar, i.e., the center of a homerange.

Symbiosis:

A number of other fish are often found in association with sharks, including free swimming fish, usually jacks (Carangids), which often surf on the bow wave in front of the shark, and remoras, or shark suckers, which attach themselves to the shark. Whenever the relationships persists, it is called *symbiosis*. If but one of the pair benefits, the relationships is called *commensalism,* whereas if both benefit it is called *mutualism.* If the symbiont benefits at the expense of the shark, the relationship is called *parasitism.* For most of the free swimming symbionts, the relationship is commensal with the shark gaining no benefit and the small fish, hitchhiking on the bow wave, taking advantage of bits of food present in the water as a consequence of the sharks feeding. These fish do not lead the shark to its prey, a common misconception which has resulted in the name pilot fish. With remoras the relationship is mutualistic as these fish, in addition to feeding on scraps or left overs, are also thought to remove parasites from the shark's body. In all cases these symbionts would appear to benefit additionally by close proximity to the shark, reducing the likelihood of predation by other creatures. Occasionally such symbionts become a nuisance to the shark, and some, e.g., the reef whitetip shark, are not uncommonly observed rolling in the sand in an attempt to dislodge or relocate an annoying remora.

A reef whitetip shark with its escort of symbiont fish: a remora, Echeneis naucrates, *and an immature golden jack,* Gnathanodon speciosus.

Enemies of the shark:

There are numerous accounts of animals having killed and sometimes fed upon sharks, including sperm whales, killer whales, pilot whales, large grouper, porpoises, sea lions and even swordfish[44][74]. It would appear, in reviewing the literature, that at least the latter three of these animals more often succumb to the shark than visa versa, and the predation upon sharks by whales is quite probably insignificant and somewhat of a rarity. The popular conception that porpoises are the shark's only natural enemy cannot be supported[28][44][73][74]. Porpoises have been observed to kill sharks by ramming them with their snouts, but usually under extenuating circumstances in aquaria or in defense of their young. More often than not, the shark is the aggressor and the victor in such encounters, and certain species, e.g., the white shark, not uncommonly feed on porpoise[44][74].

The shark's only natural enemy, of any appreciable consequence, is other sharks. Certain species, e.g., the bull shark, feed extensively on other sharks, and most large sharks will readily feed on other species. Predation of this nature is indicated by the frequent occurrence of shark flesh in the stomach contents of other sharks, and more direct evidence has been provided by underwater observation. On one occasion, in the lagoon at Rangiroa Atoll, a hammerhead, throught to be *Sphyrna mokarran,* bit in half a blackfin reef shark under what appeared to be natural conditions during the day[50]. The actual pursuit and attack were not witnessed. Only the results of the encounter were observed, wherein the head portion of a blackfin reef shark was discovered on the bottom still moving as the hammerhead closely circled. Sharks of the same species are also known to feed upon one another, and this cannibalism is not uncommon. Certain species, predominantly smaller ones, perhaps due in part to their inadequate dentition, do not appear to be cannibalistic. This is verified in some areas where such species will not take hooks baited with the flesh of their own kind[33], even though the pieces are small enough

---

The author rose early one morning to observe a large tiger shark eating the bodies of gray reef sharks caught during the night.

to be eaten. However, it is reported in this regard that there appears to be population variability. Individuals at one atoll apparently will not feed on the flesh of their own kind, while at a neighboring atoll they will partake of such bait.

man and the marauder

Man finds himself in confrontation with the shark on several fronts: (1) in direct encounters when on occasion he falls victim to attack, (2) during scientific and fishing operations where sharks cause severe economic loss in the destruction of equipment and fishing gear, (3) when for psychological reasons recreational use of the sea is curtailed, resulting in economic loss to associated industries and (4) when sharks affect fisheries by influencing the abundance and yield of some of the more desirable food resources of the sea.

Therefore, the problem presented by sharks is not a singular one. On each front the situation must be dealt with independently. Where restriction, repulsion or destruction may represent an appropriate countermeasure on some fronts, promotion of the species may be desirable on others. For example, certain sharks may, through increased numbers, serve to reduce predators which limit the abundance of desirable species. Even where restriction, repulsion or destruction seems an appropriate measure, it must be directed towards the special requirements of each category, e.g., the protection of beaches must usually be dealt with differently than the protection of divers or victims of air-sea disasters.

To the average person an encounter with a shark constitutes the ultimate fear, but the author daily confronts them to film, study and analyze their behavior. A blackfin reef shark circles while other sharks feed behind.

photo H. Löw

Shark deterrents[26]:

Short of an absolute physical barrier, the development of a single, universal deterrent effective for all species under all circumstances seems improbable. The following is a brief review of some of the various approaches to shark deterrents with comments on effectiveness and limitations.

Acoustic deterrents: This method, viewed by some as a potential universal deterrent, is only currently in the developmental stages[12]. The major obstacles to be overcome are: (1) the development of sounds repulsive to potentially dangerous species under most circumstances, including strong positive stimulus conditions, (2) overcoming the tendency of sharks to become accustomed to a novel or negative stimulus, and (3) packaging such a unit so as to be small, reliable and inexpensive enough to be of significant usefulness. In all three stages, especially the first, there are problems, e.g., repellent sounds in one situation have been observed to attract in another situation, even with the same species[49].

Electrical deterrents: Essentially the same limitations as in acoustic repellents, with the 1st step (as above) being plagued by similar problems, e.g., one apparatus tested satisfactorily repelled lemon sharks but attracted the tiger shark. However, such a device is giving good results for commercial fisheries which use it to protect nets from the ravaging of one or two particular species. The 3rd step is a significant limitation, in the use of such methods for the protection of large areas, due to the high cost of the initial installation and continued operation.

Bubble barriers: This technique was designed principally for the protection of large areas, e.g., beaches, but it has proven to be ineffective. In tests with tiger sharks, only one in 12 individuals showed any aversion to the barrier[23].

Meshing: This technique involves the placing of gill nets off beaches, and is the most effective method to date in protecting large areas. Such nets do not entirely prevent sharks from reaching beaches, as they do not form a complete barrier. Although meshing reduces the number of sharks, it does not completely eliminate potentially dangerous individuals, as evidenced by their continual capture in the nets and the observation of such individuals beyond the nets. The secret to its success has been speculated to lie in the habit of sharks to avoid areas where sharks are frequently killed[18].   However, as meshing prevents sharks from approaching beaches in a direct course and as it reduces the number of large sharks in the area, resulting in those which remain being better fed, these factors would seem at least as important in reducing attacks on protected beaches. In spite of its limited theoretical defense, meshing has proven to be most effective, dramatically reducing or eliminating incidents on otherwise attack-prone beaches. It is, however, a costly and laborious technique, only suited to beaches of appropriate configuration.

Shark screen: This deterrent was designed specifically for air-sea disaster victims. It consists essentially of a large plastic sack with flotation rings at the top. In use the flotation rings are first inflated, after which the person using it, by tipping the edge, completely fills the sack with water. In this fashion, with the individual in the sack, the stimuli normally attracting sharks under these circumstances, e.g., odor and vision, are blocked, thereby providing protection. This device is quite effective, but it must, of course, be widely distributed to persons who might find themselves in such situations to be of significant value.

Chemical repellents: Based on the observation that sharks avoid decaying shark flesh, "shark-chaser", a chemical repellent consisting of copper acetate in conjunction with a dye, was developed under the support of the U.S. Navy during WW II. It has proven limited in its effectiveness because certain species are not repelled, and even with species deterred by "shark chaser" its effectiveness is severely limited by the dilution which results from currents and the motion of waves in the sea. Some 200 chemicals have been tested[25], all with similar failings.

Poisons: Injectible poisons have been investigated as a means of protecting man[18], but sharks have been found to be extraordinarily resistant. It was found that the most effective poison was strychnine nitrate, but even a concentration sufficient to kill several horses, injected directly into free swimming sharks, took 30 seconds to 1 minute to take effect. This is considered too slow for adequate protection.

This system also required the proper implantation of the poison, and the poison itself is difficult and dangerous to handle.

Gas guns or darts: Various devices have been designed which release into the shark a gas, usually CO_2, designed to inflate the animal, thereby incapacitating it. Difficulties have been reported[20]. Due to tough hide, insufficient penetration and premature detonation are not uncommon, and this results in the gas being expelled externally. Even if proper detonation occurs, the shark must be hit in the body cavity. This requires that the diver, in order to be in proper position, must first successfully avoid the shark's jaws.

Drogues: Small parachute-type drogues have been conceived that implanted in sharks results in a drag that disrupts normal swimming. The mechanism of this system reduces its reliability, and, to a lesser degree, the location of implantation must be selected. It also seems possible that a shark so disturbed, during its struggling to free itself of the annoyance, may attack the diver.

Explosive powerheads: Delivered via spearguns, pole spears and prods, explosive powerheads have been widely experimented with. Most are prone to misfire due to wet cartriges or mechanical failure, and the danger presented to the diver by accidental detonation is generally greater than the danger presented by sharks themselves. One such weapon, however, the Sea Way Fast-Load Powerhead, promises to reduce most of these shortcomings to an acceptable level, providing the best individual diver-defense mechanism yet developed. It is the ultimate in simplistic design, and the cartrige is specially made for underwater use, eliminating misfires. It is safer in that the cartridge is only placed in the chamber when needed, and it requires a sharp impact to detonate. As the expended cartridge is automatically ejected, it is quickly reloaded, and it is quite portable.

Current developments: On the drawing board are wet suits made of material so durable that a shark's tooth cannot penetrate it, thereby reducing wounds to mere bruises. Also being experimented with is an ointment incorporating a

An aggressive blue shark meets the "fast-load" powerhead—a safe and effective diver defense weapon developed by Rhett McNair of Sea Way Hawaii, Inc. and marketed by Aqua Craft, U.S.A.

photos C. Nicklin

71

repellent chemical derived from the skin secretions of flatfish, which essentially prevents the shark from biting. Certain deterrent measures being developed will have to take into consideration the recently recognized alternative motivation causing sharks to attack man, i.e., socially derived fighting rather than feeding motivation. For example, as sounds have produced exaggerated-swimming display behavior, known to precede certain non-feeding motivated attacks, any acoustic deterrent must be evaluated for its possible effect in causing such attacks. Likewise, drogue type devices must be tested in this regard.

Shark sense: Even though deterrents have a degree of effectiveness for special situations, and will no doubt be improved upon, they will likely never find universal application. Many persons will continue to find themselves confronted by sharks without the aid of such deterrents. For such persons, one of the most effective defenses may be to become educated on the subject or in other words acquire "shark sense". This involves three basic areas of knowledge: (1) be able to identify the various species of sharks likely to be encountered in a given area and become familiar with the habits and specific behavior peculiar to these species, (2) become familiar with general behavioral patterns and learn to recognize the various motivations which are instrumental in affecting shark behavior, (3) draw upon such knowledge and apply it to shark encounters, each of which is essentially unique, having a different set of circumstances. Such knowledge is not difficult to obtain, and an understanding of the principles set forth in this book, combined with a little experience, should suffice. Native spearfishermen throughout the world obtain such an awareness through practical experience, which normally sees them through a lifetime of daily shark encounters. Many scientists and film makers have likewise acquired such awareness and daily confront sharks to obtain their desired goals.

Shark encounters, behavioral countermeasures:

Although there are about 250 species of sharks, only 30 or so

As part of the daily routine during a two year tagging study, the author baits-in, records marked individuals, and tags unmarked ones—in this case reef whitetip sharks.

are dangerous to man. Of the dozen or so species usually occuring in any given area, the majority are usually relatively harmless, and dangerous species are only occasionally common. By recognizing the species which are relatively harmless, one can feel a certain security in most shark encounters. The following is a review of some of the specific points to determine in shark encounters with recommended behavioral countermeasurers.

General rationale: Do not view the shark as unpredictable but rely upon whatever predictability can be attributed to the shark under the circumstances. However, be prepared for the unexpected.

Determine sharks motivation: Sharks do not attack without reason. Determine the stimulus attracting the shark and identify the motivation involved.

Feeding motivation: Generally identified by the shark orienting towards a specific object from which feeding stimuli, e.g., sound, odor or visual cues, are emanating. Remember, sharks are acutely equipped to determine the sources of attractant stimuli and only rarely make mistakes.

Stimulus originating from other than the individual (air-sea disaster victim, swimmer, diver): Indicated by orientation to an obvious stimulus source, e.g., speared fish being carried by the diver or fish struggling on the shaft.

Countermeasure: (1) Conservative approach: Separate oneself from the stimulus source, e.g., jettison speared fish being carried or abandon fish struggling on the shaft. (2) Alternate approach. If one is willing to accept additional risk, the fish can be defended (not recommended with sharks in excess of 2m (6 1/2 ft). As the shark is generally interested in the smaller fish constituting its normal prey, it can usually be intimidated by the larger size of the diver. Native spear-fishermen in the Tuamotus quickly pull the fish to the surface holding it out of the water, thereby reducing the sound and odor that stimulate the shark. If the shark comes close, they kick it. As strong feeding stimuli appear to

The early use of a Farallon powered cage for diver protection during feeding observations proved a bulky and unecessary precaution, especially with small sharks, e.g., the blackfin reef shark pictured.

suppress display and subsequent fighting-motivated attack, the shark, being preoccupied in obtaining a meal, will generally not become stimulated to attack in a fighting sense. However, repeated denial of the prey to the same shark, especially a gray reef shark, is reported sufficient to change its motivation, eventually eliciting display[3], at which time the only recourse is to relinquish the prey or face imminent, non-feeding motivated attack. Such attack will no longer be oriented toward the speared fish but will be directed at the diver. (3) Compromise approach: Drag speared fish behind a distance of 3 to 6 m (10 to 20 ft) while swimming to a boat or to the shore where the fish can be safely removed from the water. The continued presence of the fish in the water, producing attractant stimuli, is more likely to attract sharks, but they will at least be directing their interest to the fish rather than to the diver with blood from the fish running down his arm and dripping into the water. Moreover, the risk of eliciting non-feeding motivated attack is reduced, as diver aggression is minimal and the shark is not denied access to the prey. Even in shark-infested waters, 95% of speared fish can usually be boated.

Stimulus originating from individual: (Sharks interest casual): Generally indicated by the shark repeatedly circling, usually in response to normal auditory or visual cues.

Countermeasure: Terminate any activity which may be attractant to the shark, e.g., brisk hand-over-hand swimming and kicking of the feet, or any other activity likely to be producing unusual sounds or other attractant stimuli. Always face the shark and try to calmly remove yourself to safety. Remember that time is essential, because each passing minute permits the shark to realize that the diver represents relatively harmless and vulnerable prey. However, if one is on scuba with sufficient air, it may be worth taking a few minutes, with one's back against the most appropriate shelter available, rather than risk exposure in open water. The shark's interest may wane, in which case it will depart and the incident will be finished. However, if it returns, take the first convenient opportunity, e.g., when the shark is at the greatest distance—preferably out of sight, to move along the bottom to shore or directly under the boat. If more than one diver is present, they should arrange themselves back to back, or in a circle facing outward for ascent, so that someone is always facing the shark. If a distance must be traversed on the surface, a similar procedure is recommended. If the shark moves in close, within 1.5 to 2 m (5 to 6 1/2 ft) use any means at your disposal to make yourself as undesirable as possible. It is reported that shouting, blowing bubbles, throwing ones arms out (perhaps all simultaneously) may be effective in this regard, but direct contact with the shark in a sensitive area is probably most effective. The eyes, snout and gills are among the sensitive areas to be hit, but one should save this blow for the moment of greatest effect, e.g., using a pole spear at too great a range may only serve to convince the shark of the divers helplessness. If the shark during these close circles turns towards the diver, the time has come to use a speargun, if it has not yet been employed. Spearing a shark should be a last resort, for although most species will immediately depart or direct their rage at the shaft, certain species, e.g., the "arava", *Negaprion acutidens,* and individuals of other species, will often attack the nearest object, frequently selecting an animate one, i.e., the diver. Use a bare hand only as a last resort as a shark's hide is most abrasive, and the odor of the resultant injury may stimulate the shark to attack.

Stimulus originating from, the individual: (Shark actively interested): Indicated by the shark's interest in an injured person or diver in response to an obvious stimulus source, e.g., a bleeding wound.

Countermeasure: Take every conceivable measure to reduce or terminate stimulus continuation. As the shark is already stimulated by the diver, take any measure to repel it. If contact is made, try to poke the eyes. A knife is effective for this. Sharks have given up the attack even at this late moment.

Mistaken identity: (Sharks interest active and directed toward individual): Indicated by a shark already in close, 1 to 2 m (3 to 6ft), making active, repeated passes at the diver in an attempt to get a bite hold. This situation is usually due to the divers proximity to another stimulus source, e.g., bait or a speared fish which in its struggling has inadvertently approached the diver.

Countermeasure: Increase distance by whatever means

possible between individual and other potential stimulus source. Trying to inflict minor injury on the shark at such a moment is usually ineffectual, as during the last moments of pursuit it is normally oblivious to less than incapacitating wounds, and such action by the diver increases the risk of receiving cuts or abrasions, which are likely to result in directly stimulating the shark's interest in the diver. Therefore, unless means are at hand to seriously injure the shark, e.g., a speargun or powerhead weapon, it seems advisable to employ only those deterrent measures not likely to result in injury to the diver, e.g., kicking at it with a fin. If the shark can be held at bay for a short time, sometimes just seconds, this is often sufficient time for the shark to realize it has the wrong party. This will be indicated by the shark suddenly orienting towards the true stimulus source.

Non-feeding motivation: Generally expressed by a display posture oriented toward the diver, particularly by the gray reef shark or the galapagos shark. In other species only fragments of this display may exist, e.g., depression of the pectoral fins, hunching of the back, or strange swimming movements. Non-feeding motivated attack may occur with no observable forewarning, and it is probably, with or without warning, caused by diver behavior, e.g., pursuit, cornering or other factors as of yet undetermined.

Countermeasure: At present, complete understanding of this behavior is lacking, but it appears that any aggression on the part of the diver under such circumstances may release attack. It seems best to recommend the diver remain motionless in a relaxed position, facing the shark until it departs or increases it distance. Then, slowly move away. It may also be expedient to begin slowly moving away when the display is noted, but as the "freeze" method is that used by native spearfishermen with success[72] and cannot be mistaken as fleeing (a universal releaser of predatory attack), this latter method seems more desirable at the present. Be prepared to counter a lightning-fast attack, using the most appropriate object available. It should be short for maneuverability. If a speargun, choke down on it to a position in which it can be conveniently maneuvered. The intention, also applicable in any of the preceding close encounters, is to place a rigid barrier between the diver and

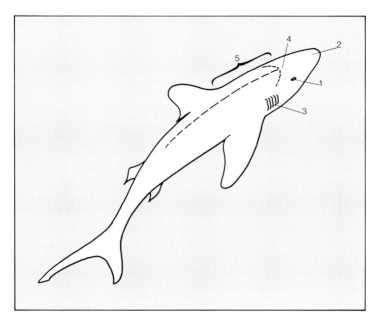

Sensitive areas on the shark towards which measures may be directed to deter aggressive individuals.
Dashed lines indicate spinal column and termination of cartilaginous skull, "chondocranium".

A. Utilizing a prod, knife or hand—the later only as a last resort (listed in order of the most sensitive areas):

1. Eye—in addition to being sensitive, it is possible to blind a shark, if for example one uses a knife effectively.

2. Snout—sensitive due to concentration of sensory systems, e.g., lateral line canals, organ of Lorenzini and sensory pits.

3. Gills—sensitive due to respiratory apparatus, e.g., concentration of blood vessels, branchial musculature and innervations.

B. Utilizing a speargun or powerhead weapon (listed in order of most effective location):

4. Directly down between the eyes through the chondocranium into the brain. A two banded arbolette is sufficient to penetrate the cartilaginous skull of a 2 m (6 ½ ft) shark, and if well placed will instantly immobilize or kill the shark.

5. Diagonally down into the spine. Best location is forward, just behind the cartilaginous skull; avoid shooting directly down through the thicker skin on the mid-dorsal line. A well placed shaft from a single banded arbolette may instantly immobilize a 2 m (6 ½ ft) shark, but the spine is more difficult to hit than the brain.

3. Gills. Shot here a shark will not be instantly immobilized, although it may eventually bleed to death. However, the forward location of the shaft impedes swimming rendering the shark less dangerous than a lateral shot further aft.

Note: shooting a shark is dangerous and can aptly be related to "catching a tiger by the tail". If not instantly immobilized, although normally fighting against the shaft, it may attack the diver.

the shark so it cannot make contact. For such use some divers carry just a short pole with them in waters where sharks may be met, and over the years this instrument has become known as the "shark billy".

Preventative measures: It is always best, of course, to take preventative measures in order to avoid confrontations. In the case of non-feeding motivated attacks, never grasp, aggress or otherwise disturb unstimulated sharks. Cornering or pursuit of unstimulated sharks is the most appropriate method known for provoking a non-feeding motivated attack.

Shark observation: Although intentionally entering the water with sharks entails a certain risk, it is often quite possible to swim among a large number of sharks, whether of the same species, or otherwise, without a significant likelihood of being attacked. If accepting the additional risk of intentionally entering the water with sharks, do so only after having acquired "shark sense". Even then, it is important to make preliminary observations of the particular population or individuals involved to see if they behave as expected. This preliminary observation should first be done from the safety of a protected position, e.g., from a boat or cage, before proceeding further. It is generally safest to observe sharks under unstimulated conditions or where sharks are satiated. It is, however, possible to bait sharks, even remaining in close proximity. This is best done where it is expected that sharks not exceeding 2 m (6 1/2 ft) will be attracted. A position up stream, if there is a current running, is essential, and shelter should be close at hand. Normally sharks so attracted will orient their attention towards the bait, paying only passing regard to the presence of divers. Quite frequently the diver's presence will inhibit sharks from aggregating or feeding upon the bait, and commonly, under such conditions, the sharks will move in close and devour the bait only after the diver departs. Such action on the part of the diver does, of course, present a degree of risk; therefore, divers should be prepared accordingly.

Confidence: Be confident in your behavior. There are indications that sharks can perceive subtleties of human behavior which may influence encounters, much as a horse can sense the ability of its rider.

However, as Jacques Yves Cousteau has noted[16] and the

author's observations have born out, it is also necessary to guard against overconfidence. The realization that man can on occasion dominate the shark and swim among them without harm, leads many a newcomer to such experiences to feel a sense of false security. Always look upon the shark with cool rationality and don't allow overconfidence to permit the development of dangerous situations.

The author's wife Chantal, observes a small gray reef shark and a reef whitetip shark feeding. **Next Page:** *A glimpse of sharks excited to the point of frenzy, but still able to discern the unprotected diver from the source of the odor.*

PART II

systematics

Sharks being fish, i.e., backboned, finned and gilled, aquatic animals, are in the animal kingdom classified under phylum Chordata, sub-phylum Vertebrata. Of the 7 classes of vertebrates, 3 are fish, the remainder being the amphibians, reptiles, birds, and mammals (see page 15). The jawless, cartilaginous fish form class Agnatha, the bony fish Osteichthyes, and the jawed, cartilaginous fish class Chondrichthyes, which includes sharks and their relatives the rays and chimeras. The chimeras, having gill slits covered by a single fold of skin, form the subclass Holocephali, while the sharks and rays, having in common multiple external gill slits, form the subclass Elasmobranchii. The Sharks form the order Selachii and the rays the order Batoidei. Sharks may in some cases resemble rays, but they can be easily distinguished by the presence of laterally, rather than ventrally located gill slits. Sharks can, therefore, simply be defined as jawed, cartilaginous fish possessing laterally located, exposed multiple gill openings. Although certainly there are other differences, this definition establishes sharks as a unique group separable from all other life forms.

Identification of families (including all those with living forms) and species (including those known or thought to occur in Polynesia).

To date, the species documented as occurring within the waters of Polynesia represent only 13 of the 21 families with living representatives. As it is probable that other species will eventually be discovered which do not fit within the families presently known to occur in this region, the following key to families includes all those known to exist in the world today. (A very recent proposal[17] has split the previously established families and if universally accepted, this will increase the number of families of living sharks.) The key continues under each family leading to identification of the 40 species, including 35 known plus 5 more thought to occur, within Polynesia. In many cases identifying the family also constitutes identification of the species, as only one species may be known within the family. However, only where this species is known, or thought to occur within the above region, will it be listed. For those identified species discussed in more detail, a page reference will immediately follow the name.

Reef whitetip shark.

Key to the living families of sharks and species ocurring in Polynesia

1. A. Anal fin present: see 2.
   B. Anal fin absent: see 16.

2. A. More than 5 pr. of gill slits: see 3.
   B. Only 5 pr. of gill openings: see 4.

3. A. Edge of first gill openings continuous under the throat, like a frilled collar ; upper and lower teeth alike in center of jaw: frill shark family CHLAMYDOSELACHIDAE.

   B. Edge of first gill opening not continuous under the throat like a frilled collar ; upper and lower teeth not alike in center of jaws: six and seven-gill shark family HEXANCHIDAE.

   1. Six gill slits present: sixgill shark, *Hexanchus griseus.*
   2. Seven gill slits present: sevengill shark, *Heptranchias perlo.*

4. A. Stout spines not preceding dorsal fins: see 5.
   B. Stout spines preceding dorsal fins: horn or bullhead shark family HETERODONTIDAE.

5. A. Two dorsal fins present: see 6.
   B. One dorsal fin present: cat shark family SCYLIORHINIDAE (in part).

6. A. Origin of pelvic fins at or behind base of 1st dorsal fin: see 9.
   B. Origin of pelvic fins at or forward of $\frac{1}{2}$ the base of the 1st dorsal fin: see 7.

7. A. Tail fin not half-moon shape; gill arches normal: see 8.
   B. Tail fin half-moon in shape ; gill arches connected by spongy, sieve-like structures: whale shark family RHINCODONTIDAE.

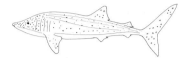

   1. Only one species in family: whale shark, *Rhincodon typus* - page 148.

8. A. No groove between nostril and mouth, but, if so, no barbel at the forward margin: cat shark family (remainder) SCYLIORHINIDAE.

   1. Shape of scales distinct: closely packed, minute, with single, pointed, slender, spine: *Apristurus spongiceps.* Single specimen known from vicinity of Bird Island, Hawaii from deep water 570 to 1,460 m (1,870 to 4,790 ft).
   B. Deep groove between nostril and mouth with a barbel at forward margin: carpet, nurse and wobbegong shark family ORECTOLOBIDAE.

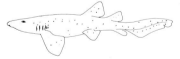

   1. Numerous species world wide, but only one species reported to occur in Polynesia: Indo-Pacific nurse shark, *Nebrius concolor* - page144.

9. A. Head not expanded laterally: see 10.
   B. Head expanded laterally and hammer shaped: hammerhead shark family SPHYRNIDAE.

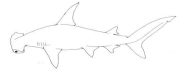

1. a. Narrowest longitudinal dimension of the head divisible into width of the head at least 3 times: see 9-B-2.
   b. Narrowest longitudinal dimension of the head divisible into width of the head less than 3 times: (possible undescribed species) squarehead hammerhead shark, *Sphyrna* sp. - page 158.
2. a. Apex of 1st dorsal fin over or forward of termination of free rear tip of same fin: see 9-B-3.
   b. Apex of 1st dorsal fin behind termination of free rear tip of same fin (behind by about the lenght of the free rear tip of this fin): great hammerhead, *Sphyrna mokarran* - page 156.
3. a. Front margin of 1st dorsal fin about equal in lenght to front margin of lower lobe of tail fin ; leading margin of head with notch at center line: scalloped hammerhead shark, *Sphyrna lewini* - page 152.
   b. Front margin of 1st dorsal fin longer than front margin of lower lobe of tail fin (by 1/3 or more) ; leading margin of head lacking notch at center line: smooth hammerhead shark, *Sphyrna zygaena.*

10. A. Tail fin not half-moon in shape: see 12.
   B. Tail fin half-moon in shape: see 11.

11. A. Teeth minute and numerous (more than 500): basking shark family CETORHINIDAE.

   B. Teeth large and few (less than 500): mako, porbeagle and white shark family LAMNIDAE.

   1. a. Last gill slit shorter than preceding 4 and generally less than $^1/_2$ the vertical height of the body ; teeth broadly trian-gular and serrated: white shark, *Carcharodon carcharias.*
      b. Last gill slit about equal in length to preceding 4 and generally more than $^1/_2$ the height of the body ; teeth narrow, long and not serrated: see 11-B-2.
   2. a. Length of the pectoral fin about 3/4 the length between snout and origin of the pectoral fin: short-finned mako, *Isurus oxyrinchus* - page 142.
      b. Length of pectoral fin about equal to the length between snout and origin of pectoral fin: long-finned mako, *Isurus paucus.*

12. A. Tail fin much longer than base of 1st dorsal fin: see 13.
   B. Tail fin shorter than base of 1st dorsal fin: false cat shark family PSEUDOTRIAKIDAE.

   1. Two species in the family and only one in the Pacific: Pacific false cat shark, *Pseudotriakis acrages.*

13. A. Tail fin much shorter than the body: see 14.
   B. Tail fin nearly as long as the entire body: thresher shark family ALOPIIDAE.

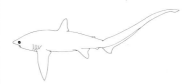

   1. a. Head without prominent crest ; base of 1st dorsal fin termination forward of pelvic fin origin; eye almost circular: common thresher shark, *Alopias vulpinus* - page 94.
      b. Head with prominent crest ; base of 1st dorsal fin termination almost over origin of pelvic fins ; eye elongated vertically: bigeye thresher shark, *Alopias superciliosus.*

14. A. 5th gill opening over or behind the front of the pectoral fin ; eye with nictitating membrane: see 21.
   B. 5th gill opening well in front of pec-

toral fin ; eye lacks nictitating membrane: see 15.

15. A. Greatly elongated snout: goblin shark family SCAPANORHYNCHIDAE.

    B. Normal snout: sand shark family ODONTASPIDAE.

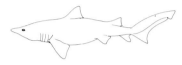

      1. Eyes large (horizontal diameter about twice as long as the largest tooth); teeth without denticles at base ; small in size to about 1 m (39 in) and usually taken deep offshore: offshore sand shark, *Odontaspis kamoharai.*
      2. Eye normal ; teeth with denticles on each side of base ; size to around 3 m (10 ft): inshore sand shark, *Odontaspis ferox.*

16. A. Snout normal: see 17.
    B. Snout saw-like, very long with sharp teeth on edges and long fleshy barbels: sawshark family PRISTIOPHORIDAE.

17. A. Pectoral fins not overlapping gill slits ; body cylindrical ; eyes on side of head: see 18.
    B. Pectoral fins wing-like ; body flattened ; eyes on top of head: angel shark family SQUATINIDAE.

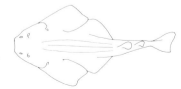

18. A. A spine present at front margins of both 1st and 2nd dorsal fins (if not visable, broken or embedded spines easily apparent to the touch): see 19.
    B. 1st dorsal fin (usually) and 2nd dorsal fins (always) lacking spine: see 20.

19. A. Each row of upper teeth consecutively increased in number by one, resulting in a triangular patch ; body approximately triangular in cross section with a prominent ridge on each lower side: family OXYNOTIDAE.

    B. Each row of upper teeth with similar numbers ; body approximately circular in cross section with no more than a weak ridge between pelvic and pectoral fins: spiny dogfish family SQUALIDAE.

      1. a. Teeth of upper jaw with several cusps: see 19-B-2.
         b. Teeth of upper jaw with only one cusp: Blainville's dogfish shark, *Squalus blainvillei.*
      2. a. Shape of teeth in upper and lower jaws similar, with 3 or more narrow cusps: granular shark, *Centroscyllium granulosum.*
         b. Shape of teeth dissimilar in upper and lower jaws ; upper teeth with 3 or more cusps and lower teeth flattened and broad, with a single inclined cusp: Hawaiian shark, *Etmopterus villosus.*

20. A. Teeth with several cusps, alike in both jaws: bramble shark family ECHINORHINIDAE.

1. The several world wide species are possibly one:
   a. Scales large, 15 mm (5/8 in) wide on 2 m (6 ft, 6 in) specimen ; potential world wide species: bramble shark, *Echinorhinus brucus.*
   b. Scales smaller, 4 mm ($^1/_2$ in) wide; possibly distinct species: prickly shark, *Echinorhinus cookei.*
B. Teeth with single cusp, not alike in both jaws: family DALATIIDAE.

   1. a. Base of 2nd dorsal fin more than twice as long as base of 1st dorsal fin: slime shark, *Euprotomicrus bispinatus.*
      b. Base of 2nd dorsal fin only slightly longer than base of 1st dorsal fin: cigar shark, *Isistius brasiliensis.*

21. A. Teeth with 3 or more cusps, low, rounded and normally in a mosaic arrangement: smooth dogfish and smooth hound family TRIAKIDAE.

B. Teeth with only 1 major cusp, bladelike and lacking mosaic arrangement: requiem or gray shark family CARCHARHINIDAE.

   1. a. Caudal keel absent: see 21-B-2.
      b. Caudal keel present: tiger shark, *Galeocerdo cuvier* - page 126.
   2. a. Upper precaudal pit present ; spircles reduced or absent: see 21-B-3.
      b. Precaudal pits absent ; spiracles prominent: soupfin shark, *Galeorhinus zyopterus.*
   3. a. Teeth unicuspid: see 21-B-4.
      b. Teeth multicuspid, with smaller sharp cusps on one or both sides of the main cusp: reef whitetip shark, *Triaenodon obesus* - page 136.
   4. a. 2nd dorsal fin less than 1/3 as large as 1st dorsal fin: see 21-B-5.
      b. 2nd dorsal fin nearly as large as 1st dorsal fin: South Pacific lemon shark, *Negaprion acutidens* - page 132.
   5. a. 1st dorsal fin further forward, midpoint of its base closer to rear end of base of pectoral fins than to origin of pelvic fins, or about equal distance from both points ; body gray or brown but not blue (genus Carcharhinus): see 21-B-6.
      b. 1st dorsal fin far back, midpoint of its base closer to origin of pelvic fins than to rear end of base of pectoral fins ; body dark blue: blue shark, *Prionace glauca.*
   6. a. A longitudinal ridge present on the middle of the back between the two dorsal fins (a notable ridge in the deeper epidermal tissue): see 21-B-10.
      b. Back smooth, no ridge between the two dorsal fins (sometimes a visual line or slight seam is present): see 21-B-7.
   7. a. Snout very blunt or broadly rounded, U-Shaped: see 21-B-8.
      B. Snout pointed, V-shaped: see 21-B-9.
   8. a. Tips of most fins abruptly jet black: blackfin reef shark, *Carcharhinus melanopterus* - page 122.
      b. Tips of fins not black: bull shark, *Carcharhinus leucas* - page 112.
   9. a. Lower teeth not serrated ; rear margin and lower lobe of tail fin conspicuously dark ; first dorsal fin without a black tip: gray reef shark, *Carcharhinus amblyrhynchos* - page 100.
      b. Lower teeth serrated (a magnifying lens is sometimes needed to see the serrations) ; all fins with black

tips (especially prominent in smaller individuals); in larger individuals the black is sometimes faded or restricted to a few centimeters (about an inch) at the termination of the fin -common in Tuamotu specimens—except for the undersides of the pectorals fins, which remain prominently black tipped): blacktip shark, *Carcharhinus limbatus* - page 114.

10. a. 1st dorsal fin, and usually pectoral fins with white tips: see 21-B-11.

   b. Fins without white tips: see 21-B-12.

11. a. Apex of 1st dorsal fin broadly rounded, its tip white but mottled with tiny dark spots ; 2nd dorsal fin usually with dark markings: oceanic whitetip shark, *Carcharhinus longimanus* - page 118.

   b. Apex of 1st dorsal fin pointed ; tips of dorsal, pectoral and tail fins white, not mottled with black ; 2nd dorsal fin without dark markings: silvertip shark, *Carcharhinus albimarginatus* - page 96.

12. a. Nostrils with a distinct, finger-like lobe ; distance from snout tip to mouth notably greater than width of mouth (may be nearly equal to mouth width in very large individuals); snout moderatly pointed: bignose shark, *Carcharhinus altimus.*

   b. Nostrils without a finger-like lobe ; distance from snout tip to mouth about equal to or (usually) less than width of mouth ; *(C. obscurus* rarely has a short, finger-like lobe on the nostril, but its snout is short and rounded): see 21-B-13.

13. a. Length of free rear tip of 2nd dorsal fin not greater than twice the height ; snout broadly rounded: see 21-B-14.

   b. Length of free rear tip of 2nd dorsal fin more than twice height of fin; snout moderatley pointed: silky shark, *Carcharhinus falciformis* - page 106.

14. a. Origin of 1st dorsal fin about over inner posterior corner of pectoral fins: see 21-B-15.

   b. Origin of 1st dorsal fin over rear end of base (not the inner posterior corner) of pectoral fins: sandbar shark, *Carcharhinus plumbeus.*

15. a. 2nd dorsal fin low, rear margin nearly straight ; 1st dorsal fin low and broad, front-margin shaped like an arc of a circle: dusky shark, *Carcharhinus obscurus.*

   b. 2nd dorsal fin relatively high, its rear margin highly concave ; 1st dorsal fin high and erect, front margin nearly straight: galapagos shark, *Carcharhinus galapensis* - page 110.

The white shark, known by many aliases, e.g., great white, white death, maneater, etc. may occur in all waters of the world.

This species is reported to produce small litters, one account listing 9 pups of about 2 ft (60 cm) length. The white shark is thought to mature at a length between 11 and 14 ft. (around 4 m), and it is the world's largest living predatory fish. Although there exists a dubious early account of this species measured at 36 ft (11 m), one of the largest reliable accounts is that of a 21 ft (6 m), 7,302 lb (3,320 kg) specimen taken off Cuba in the 1940's. Inspite of its relative rarity, this species holds the dubious record of being responsible for the greatest number of authenticated attacks on man. Although on a single encounter basis the white shark is likely the world's most dangerous, persons have on several occasions met this animal underwater without being attacked. Still others have survived the terrible grip of this formidable shark's jaws.

Global distribution of Polynesian Sharks

A guide to distribution throughout the world of species known or thought to occur in Polynesia.

Combination alphabetical and numerical code (left margin) indicates approximate species distribution on global map. Alphabetical code (right margin) indicates distribution within Polynesia: C = Cook Islands, F.P. = French Polynesia, H = Hawaiian Islands, A = all three islands groups, and? = suspected occurrence. (Note: global distribution is frequently influenced by seasonal warming of currents carrying warm tropical waters into temperate zones (arrows indicate currents); hence, basically tropical species penetrate certain temperate areas accounting for their inclusion in such regions. Moreover, certain species may be rare in the region indicated, and overlapping, even beyond that indicated, can be expected.

NORTH TEMPERATE

TROPICAL

A : 1, 2
B : 1, 2, 3, 4,
8, 9, 10,
15, 16
C : 1, 2
D : 1
E : 1, 2
F : 1, 2
H : 1—

SOUTH TEMPERATE

A : 1, 2
B : 1, 2, 4, 5
C : 1
E : 1, 2
F : 1, 2
L : 3

EASTERN ATLANTIC   INDIAN OCEAN

A. *Alopiidae:* thresher shark family.
   1. *Alopias superciliosus,* (Lowe, 1840)   Bigeye thresher shark   A ?
   2. *A. vulpinus,* (Bonnaterre, 1788)   Common Thresher shark   A

B. *Carcharhinidae:* requeim or gray shark family.
   1. *Carcharhinus albimarginatus,* (Rüppel, 1835)   Silvertip shark   C.F.P.
   2. *C. altimus,* (Springer, 1950)   Bignose shark   H
   3. *C. amblyrhynchos,* (Bleeker, 1856)   Gray reef shark   A
   4. *C. falciformis,* (Bibron in Müller & Henle, 1841)   Silky shark   C ?, F.P., H
   5. *C. galapagensis,* (Snodgrass & Heller, 1905)   Galapagos shark   A
   6. *C. leucas,* (Valenciennes in Müller & Henle, 1841) Bull shark   F.P.
   7. *C. limbatus,* (Valenciennes in Müller & Henle, 1841) Blacktip shark   C ?, F.P., H
   8. *C. longimanus,* (Poey, 1861)   Oceanic Whitetip shark A
   9. *C. melanopterus,* (Quoy & Gaimard, 1824)   Blackfin reef shark   A
  10. *C. obscurus,* (Lesueur, 1818)   Dusky shark   A ?
  11. *C. plumbeus,* (Valenciennes in Nardo, 1827)   Sandbar shark   H
  12. *Galeorhinus zyopterus,* (Jordan & Gilbert, 1883) Soupfin shark   H
  13. *Galeocerdo cuvier,* (Peron & Lesueur, 1822)   Tiger shark   A
  14. *Negaprion acutidens,* (Rüppel, 1835)   South Pacific lemon shark F.P.
  15. *Prionace glauca,* (Linnaeus, 1758)   Blue shark   C ?, F.P. ?,
  16. *Triaenodon obesus,* (Rüppel, 1835)   Reef whitetip shark   A

C. *Dalatiidae:*
   1. *Euprotomicrus bispinatus,* (Quoy & Gaimard, 1824) Slime shark   C ?, F.P. ?,
   2. *Isistius brasiliensis,* (Quoy & Gaimard, 1824)   Cigar shark   C ?, F.P. ?,

D. *Echinorhinidae:* bramble shark family
   1. *Echinorhinus brucus,* (Bonnaterre, 1788)   Bramble shark   A ?
   2. *E. cookei,* (Pietschmann, 1928)   Prickly shark   C ?, F.P. ?,

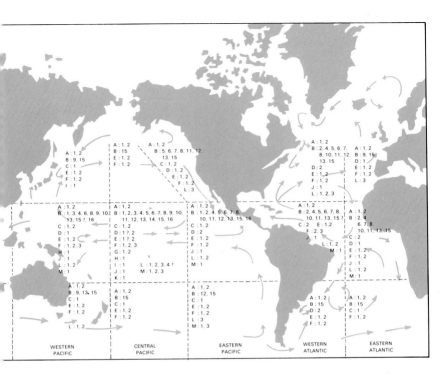

E. **Hexanchidae:** six or seven gill shark family
   1. *Heptranchias perlo,* (Bonnaterre, 1788) — Sevengill shark — A ?
   2. *Hexanchus griseus,* (Bonnaterre, 1788) — Sixgill shark — C ?, F.P. ?. H
F. **Lamnidae:** mako, porbeagle & white shark family
   1. *Carcharodon carcharias,* (Linnaeus, 1758) — White shark — C ?, F.P. ?, H
   2. *Isurus oxyrinchus,* (Rafinesque, 1810) — Short-finned mako, shark — A
   3. *I. paucus,* (Guitart-Manday, 1966) — Long-finned mako, shark — C ?, F.P. ?. H
G. **Odontaspidae:** sand shark family
   1. *Odontaspis ferox,* (Risso, 1810) — Inshore sand shark — H
   2. *O. kamoharai,* (Matsubara, 1936) — Offshore sand shark — H
H. **Orectolobidae:** capet, nurse & wobbegong family
   1. *Nebrius concolor,* (Rüppell, 1835) — Indo-Pacific nurse shark — C, F.P.
I. **Pseudotriakidae:** false cat shark family
   1. *Pseudotriakis acrages* (Jordan & Snyder, 1904) — Pacific false cat shark — H
J. **Rhincodontidae:** whale shark family
   1. *Rhincodon typus,* (Smith, 1829) — Whale shark — A
K. **Scyliorhinidae:** cat shark family
   1. *Apristurus spongiceps,* (Gilbert, 1905) — Deep-water cat shark — H
L. **Sphyrnidae:** hammerhead shark family
   1. *Sphyrna lewini,* (Griffith & Smith, 1834) — Scalloped hammerhead — A
   2. *S. Mokarran,* (Rüppel, 1835) — Great hammerhead — C ?, F.P.
   3. *S. zygaena,* (Linnaeus, 1758) — Smooth hammerhead — C ?, H
   4. *S.* sp. (potentially unidentified species) — Squarehead hammerhead — F.P. ?
M. **Squalidae:** spiny dogfish family
   1. *Centroscyllium granulosum,* (Gunther, 1880) — Granular shark — C ?, F.P. ?, H
   2. *Etmopterus villosus,* (Gilbert, 1905) — Hawaiian shark — H
   3. *Squalus blainvillci,* (Risso, 1826) — Blainville's dogfish shark — H

93

Sharks of French Polynesia

ALOPIIDAE

ALOPIAS VULPINUS
(Bonnaterre, 1788),
MAO AERO
COMMON THRESHER SHARK[4]

Synonyms: Although known by numerous common names, fox shark—derived from the scientific name—is probably the second most widely used. The Greeks called this shark *alopex* and the Romans *vulpes,* both meaning fox, used not only because of this shark's extraordinarily long tail, but also because of its reputed cunning.

Color: Basically dark above and near white below, this species varies in color between grey to blue-green.

Morphology: The upper lobe of the tail is greatly elongated, nearly equaling the length of the body—a diagnostic feature of each of the 6 or so described members of this family. The lower precaudal pit is present in some individuals and lacking in others. The pelvic and first dorsal fins are about equal in size. The eye is basically circular. This species approaches the 6m (20ft) range, and just under 1/2 the length is the tail. Nonetheless, it is a big shark, for the International Game Fishing Association all tackle record (not measured) weighed 420 kg (922 lbs).

Distribution: This species is found around the world from temperate to tropical seas. Its poleward limits to the north include Ireland and New England, on the east coast of the U.S., and Oregon, on the west coast. Its southernmost excursions include South Africa, Western Australia and Queensland. These limits are exceeded by some individuals.

Habitat: The common thresher is generally pelagic—an inhabitant of the open sea; however, it is occasionally found inshore and is even reported to enter the larger atoll lagoons in the Tuamotus[3]. In the tropics this species usually inhabits deep water, 300 m (1,000 ft).

Reproduction: This species is probably not sexually mature at much less than 4.2 m (14 ft). Litters are small, usually 2 to 4, but the pups are often large, 1.5 m (5ft).

Feeding: The common thresher reportedly feeds only on fish, generally smaller types, e.g., flying fish, smelt, etc. Its common name is derived by its habit of using the tail to thrash the water while herding small fish into position to feed upon them. Although

The thresher, notable for its elongated tail, also has long pectoral fins and large eyes common to many pelagic, deep water species. The small mouth is equipped with 21 or 22 small triangular teeth on each side of the upper jaw. The 3rd tooth either side of center is smaller than the 2nd and the 4th.

once doubted by prominent ichthyologists, it now seems beyond question that the thresher also uses the tail to injure or kill prey. Numerous observations of fish, and even one of a sea bird, having been killed in such a manner have been recorded over the years. In the Cook islands, fishermen fear its tail more than its jaws[72], inferring that the tail is used defensively and that the thrashing is directed against it captors. This species is one of the few known to take a moving bait, which accounts for its occasional capture during fishing activities. Upon being hooked, it reportedly has the cunning to swim up the line, biting it off above the wire leader.

Disposition: Although sometimes large, the thresher is not known to attack man. In the water, divers and swimmers are apparently avoided, for although uncommon, even fewer are seen than might be expected. The author had the rare opportunity to see a thresher which had been attracted to an underwater speaker, during acoustic experiments off the coast of Southern California. This individual, although obviously interested in the sound being transmitted, was quite wary and departed after circling widely with an eye apparently on the observer at the surface.

CARCHARHINUS ALBIMARGINATUS
(Rüppell, 1835)
TAPETE
SILVERTIP SHARK[41]

Synonyms: This shark was previously known under the scientific name *C. platyrhynchus* and also under the common name of whitetip reef shark, which has fallen into disuse because of confusion with another species, the reef whitetip shark, *Triaenodon obesus*. The silvertip is known as the *arava* in the Cook Islands[72], the same name given to *N. acutidens* in French Polynesia.

Color: The silvertip is generally dark gray, sometimes with a brownish cast above, fading to white below. Diagnostic are the whitetips on both the upper and lower lobes of the tail and on the tips of the first dorsal and pectoral fins which extend as a white margin along the trailing edges. Less noticeable white tips are also present on the trailing edges of the second dorsal and anal fins.

Morphology: This species possesses an interdorsal ridge; rounded snout of medium length; first dorsal fin height less than length of base; and second dorsal less than 1/2 the height of the first dorsal. The silvertip is unlikely to reach much over 3 m (10ft); 2.61 m and 2.75 m (8ft 7in & 9ft) are the sizes of two of the larger specimens recorded.

Distribution: The silvertip is widespread in warm tropical and sub-tropical water from the Galapagos and Revill Gigedos Islands in the Eastern Pacific,

The silvertip's unique color pattern renders the species both unmistakable and beautiful. The white fin margins are accentuated in some individuals by stark contrast with a nearly black body. Other individuals may have a lighter body, but even then the white fin margins are clearly visible.

photo P. Schaller

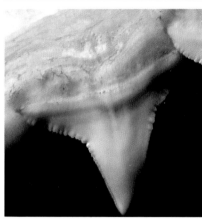

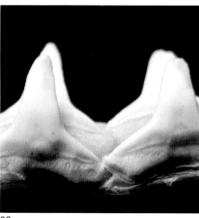

through French Polynesia and the Marshall Islands to South Africa and the Natal Coast. In the Indian Ocean, it is the most abundant shark around Mauritius and the Seychelles. It is conspicuously absent in Hawaii and does not occur in the Atlantic.

Habitat: The silvertip is generally a deeper inshore shark, inhabiting the waters from 30 to 400 m (100 to 1,300 ft) along drop-offs and banks. Small individuals are sometimes found in atoll lagoons of the Tuamotus. Although generally bottom oriented, the silvertip has been found far out at sea, and it is not infrequently found near the surface—usually as a result of attractive stimulus conditions. They also occur at sea in depths approaching the above maximum, where the bottom is much deeper.

Reproduction: Maturity is reached between 1.65 and 1.80 m (5ft 5in and 5ft 11in) for males and a little longer for females—one of the smallest pregnant silvertips recorded being 1.99 m (6ft 6in). Breeding appears to be seasonal. In Mauritius and the Seychelles it occurs in December and January. Other Indian Ocean and Tuamotu data fit this pattern. As the gestation period is around 12 months, the breeding season occurs with pupping. The young number up to 11 per litter, 5 or 6 being usual. The sex ratio is 1:1, and pups are born at a length of 50 to 80 cm (20 to 32in). **Feeding**: One study shows stomach contents as being 70% smallish fish, e.g. flying fish (Exocoetidae), lantern fish (Myctophidae) and sole (Soleidae).

Dentition: $\frac{13\text{-}1\ or\ 2\text{-}\ 13}{12\text{-}1\ or\ 2\text{-}\ 12}$ *Teeth in upper and lower jaws dissimilar, but cusps of all serrate. Serrations of lower teeth in young specimens difficult to observe with the naked eye.*

Opposite: *A hooked silvertip allows close observation of this not often easily observed species.*

10% eagle ray, *Aetobatis narinari*; 10% octopus and the balance indigestible material. This indicates that the silvertip possesses a fairly generalized feeding pattern, being able to feed from flat fish on the bottom to mid-water and surface fish. When feeding in the presence of an observer, the silvertip usually watches from a distance, grabbing the prey in a rapid dash at an opportune moment after which it glides away. Occasionally, especially in younger specimens, this species is curious and closely approaches divers.

Disposition: The silvertip has been said to attack man, and its large size, strong dentition and inquisitive and persistent nature make it a potentially dangerous species. To a degree it is a nervous shark, remaining at the edge of any disturbance, but if attracted, it becomes persistent, gradually moving closer. The author spent more than 30 minutes in the water with an individual approaching the maximum size under strong baited conditions. At first the shark turned away when some 15m (50ft) distant, but after some time, this shark came closer than 2m (6 1/2ft) and even pursued the diver during his exit into 3m (10ft) of water near the surf. This species shows a strong attraction to certain artificially produced, low-frequency, pulsed sounds during acoustic experiments, which may relate to their reported attraction to ships at sea.

CARCHARHINUS AMBLYRHYNCHOS
(Bleeker, 1856)
RAIRA
GRAY REEF SHARK[71]

Synonyms: There are many, but the most recent by which the species was commonly known is *C. menisorrah*—also known as *C. nesiotes*. The recent name change and confusion with other species has resulted in the recommended common name of long-nosed blacktail shark, which may become established upon acceptance of a pending revision of the genus. Regarding local names, the species is known in the Gambiers as *mago ki-riiaura*[3] and in the Cook Islands as *papera*[72].

Color: As the name implies, this species is a basic gray color on the upper portions of the body, fading smoothly to white on the belly and underparts. A characteristic feature of coloration is the broad band of black on the trailing edge of the tail, especially prominent on the lower lobe. This black band fades forward into the basic gray body color, and does not have a precise demarcation as in certain other species. The second dorsal, anal, pelvics, and tips on the undersides of pectoral fins are also pigmented black. The first dorsal fin is never tipped or fringed with black, but it may occasionally have a slight white edge.

Morphology: Although sometimes possessing a slight but distinct visual line between the dorsal fins, this species does not possess the raised interdorsal ridge common to other species. Its maximum recorded size is 2.33 m (7ft 7 3/4in); however, individuals over 1.9 m (6ft 3in) are rare.

The gray reef shark is characterized by the black trailing edge on the tail and a lack of fin tip coloration—except rarely for a fine white margin on the 1st dorsal.

Distribution: The gray reef shark occurs in tropical and sub-tropical waters from the Hawaiian chain and Easter Island westward to the western Indian Ocean. It is reported from as far north as Midway (28°N) southward to Easter Island (28°S)[71].

Habitat: The gray reef shark generally seems to prefer rugged terrain such as that on the drop-off of outer reefs and in lagoons around patch reefs in or arising from deeper water. It often shows a preference for areas adjacent to strong currents, e.g., the ocean and lagoon sides of atoll passes. This species shows a definite orientation towards the bottom, although it not infrequently rises to the surface. Telemetry tagging data exists[37] which indicates it may swim kilometers (miles) off shore at a depth of less than 100 m (330ft), while the bottom may be a thousand meters (over 3,000ft) below. In the central Pacific it is the most common deeper, inshore shark, and is found from the surface to a little over 100 m (330ft). Where the reef blackfin shark is absent, e.g., Johnston and Marcus Islands, the gray reef shark is found commonly by day over the shallow reef normally reserved for the blackfin reef shark. However, at Toau in the Tuamotus where the blackfin reef shark is abundant, the gray reef shark is occasionally found by day in 1 m (39in) of water. The gray reef shark is usually restricted to small islands, where it shows a preference for the leeward side[71]. In keeping with the above generalization, the gray reef shark is uncommon around the major Society and Hawaiian Islands, but is abundant in the Tuamotu Islands and leeward Hawaiian chain.

Reproduction: The gray reef shark is viviparous. Its gestation period lasts about 12 months. The number of

pups per litter range up to 6, generally born at a length of about 45 to 60 cm (18 to 24in). The sex ratio at birth is 1:1. Information on the mating season is incomplete and somewhat contradictory, but it would appear that a generalized season or two exist between November and April in both Northern and Southern Hemispheres.

Growth[71]: Individuals tagged, measured, released and recaptured at later date have provided growth data. The gray reef shark in the sea appears to grow at the rate of about 22 mm

102

13/16 in) per year, while in captivity they grow at twice this rate.

Age[71]: Through tooth replacement studies and indirect calculations, estimates of age are possible. Based on these studies, the gray reef shark appears to mature at between 7 and 7 1/2 years, females maturing slightly earlier than males. Estimation of longevity is less accurate, but studies indicate that the gray reef shark lives to about 25 years of age.

Feeding: One report,[71] which is probably a good average, indicates that

The notable packing behavior of gray reef sharks, juveniles pictured, is indicative of their basic social nature.

the gray reef shark feeds 53 % of the time on small fish (under 30 cm (12in), 25% on larger fish, 18% on cephalopods (squid and octopus) and 4% on crustaceans (crab, lobster and shrimp). This species is only very rarely cannibalistic, although it will eat the flesh of closely related species. The gray reef shark, although capable of feeding off the bottom, is most successful in feeding on organisms in

103

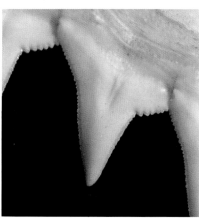

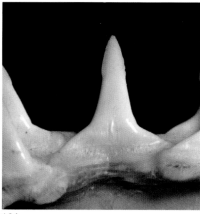

the water column near the bottom. It can rapidly follow odors to their source for substantial distances (at least hundreds of meters (yards), and it is capable of directly determining the source of sounds for a distance of about 200 m (650ft).

Activity[37]: During the day, gray reef sharks frequently assemble in packs in routine locations, sometimes just a point along outer reefs, pass entrances or in lagoons—commonly adjacent to a pass. At night, although some individuals may go in the same direction, there seems to be a dispersal and various patterns of movement. Some individuals move into passes, while others range in the lagoon or travel to another pass. Although active by day, the gray reef shark appears to be a predominantly nocturnal species. Packing behavior is especially prevalent in juveniles which form close knit groups in areas considered pupping grounds.

Disposition: Under unstimulated conditions, unlike most inshore sharks, the gray reef shark is innately curious, especially in remote areas not frequently visited by divers. A slow moving sailing craft, skirting reef drop-offs in remote areas, is often sufficient to attract this shark to the surface from its normal haunts near the bottom. A diver entering the water may attract the attention of 5 or 10 individuals at a time, which may pass as close as 1 m (about 3ft). Fortunately, these sharks become accustomed to divers rapidly and within 15 min-

Dentition: $\frac{13 \text{ to } 15 \text{ -1 or 2- } 13 \text{ to } 15}{12 \text{ to } 14 \text{ -1 or 2- } 12 \text{ to } 14}$ with $\frac{14 \text{ -1- } 14}{14 \text{ -1- } 14}$ being average. Teeth in upper and lower jaws dissimilar and the tips of lower teeth often enlarged—slightly arrowhead like; uppers serrate and lowers not serrate.

Opposite: The gray reef shark is an inquisitive species.

utes there may no longer be a single shark visible. Only occasionally, during subsequent days at the same location, will a shark again be observed. Under stimulated conditions, the gray reef shark can become very aggressive and is potentially quite dangerous. When feeding stimuli are present, especially during spearfishing activities where all the major senses are stimulated, the gray reef shark is strongly motivated to attack. Normally, it is quite able to discriminate the source of the stimuli. This results in the shark—often in competition with others—directing its attack towards the speared fish, ripping it off the shaft. This behavior is especially prevalent in remote areas where sharks have not learned to disregard or even fear native divers, who often spear troublesome individuals. Although the gray reef shark is normally adept at perceiving the source of feeding stimuli, occasionally this shark may mistakenly bite a diver, especially if, for example, a speared fish in its struggling closely approaches the diver. As a consequence of this behavior, and perhaps the one described below, in the Tuamotus where local inhabitants spear fish as a major source of their livelihood, the gray reef shark is responsible for more attacks on man than any other species. It has accounted for at least 10 injurious assaults and one fatality in the past decade[3].

The gray reef shark attacks for non-feeding reasons in a mode more closely related to fighting behavior[6 7 8 34 36]. (see Aggressive Behaviour, Dominance and Territoriality). Fortunately, this species normally enters into a prominent defensive threat display or posture, warning a diver that an attack may be forth-coming, and in view of such warning, a diver can usually prevent this type of attack by terminating his aggressiveness or other aggravating behavior towards the shark.

CARCHARHINUS FALCIFORMIS
(Bibron in Müller & Henle, 1841)
TAUTUKAU
SILKY SHARK[4]

Synonyms: Scientifically this shark has been known as *C. malpeloensis* and *C. floridanus.* In the Eastern Pacific it is colloquially known as the net-eater shark.

Color: This shark lacks a distinctive color pattern, being medium to dark gray above and fading to white below. The first dorsal may be paler in color, and the second dorsal, anal and lower caudal may have dusky but not conspicuous tips.

Morphology: The most diagnostic features are elongated, free rear margins on the second dorsal and anal fins, the former being twice the length of the fin height. This species possesses a notable interdorsal ridge, and the 1st dorsal origin is behind the inner pectoral corner. Maximum size is just over 3m (10ft), one of the largest recorded being 3.05 m (10ft even).

Distribution: The silky shark is found in warm waters of all three major oceans. It is common between 10° North and South in the Eastern Pacific, being the most abundant offshore shark in that area. It was found recently in the Tuamotus[38], and it has been found as far as 26° South off the Mozambique coast.

Habitat: The silky shark is basically pelagic, becoming more abundant toward land, which has resulted in its being termed semi-pelagic in some areas, e.g., the Western Atlantic. It is generally found on or near the surface, but it has been taken as deep as about 500 m (1,600ft).

The otherwise plain silky shark may be identified by the very long free rear tip on the second dorsal fin—twice as long as the fin is high.

photo D. Nelson

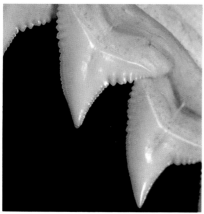

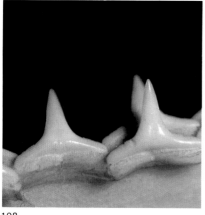

photo D. Nelson

Dentition: $\frac{16 \cdot 2 \cdot 16}{16 \cdot 2 \cdot 16}$ *is usual. Teeth small for the size of the shark and dissimilar in each jaw. Uppers usually heavily serrate at the base.*

Reproduction: This species matures at a length somewhat over 2.0 m (6 1/2ft)—a mature Atlantic male has been recorded measuring 2.18 m (7ft 2in). Data do not indicate a specific breeding season, and the gestation period is unknown. Litters range up to 14 in number, with the average varying geographically—being 11 off Madagascar and around 6 in the Central Pacific. In the Western Atlantic, pupping grounds occur on the rim of the continental shelf and oceanic banks (Western Caribbean)

photo D. Nelson

Left: A diver decends to tag an unsuspecting silky shark—the species generally being uninhibited and easily worked with. **Top**: *Once implanted a conventional tag readily permits individual recognition.*

in depths of 80 to 100 m (about 300ft).

Feeding: Stomach contents vary from crabs, octopus, squid, and other inshore fish to pelagic bait fish and even tuna, indicating rather generalized feeding habits. The commonest pattern, seems to involve feeding on smaller bait fish. This species is frequently attracted to various low-frequency sounds during acoustic investigations.

Disposition: The silky is generally a calm and cautious species, usually moving in a consistent graceful manner. The author has swum for several days with several dozen individuals present at one time, under unbaited and baited conditions, and found that this species pays little attention to divers. Spearing fish in the presence of this species, however, abruptly releases rapid food seeking behavior. Silkies do not hesistate to remove speared fish from the shaft, but even under such circumstances, they still pay little attention to the diver. Upon first encounter with a diver this species can become aggressive, and due to their size and capacity to inflict serious injury, they should be regarded as potentially dangerous.

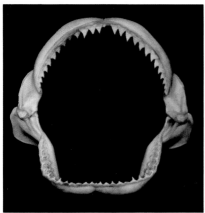

CARCHARHINUS GALAPAGENSIS
(Snodgrass & Heller, 1905)
UNKNOWN (probably not distinguished from *RAIRA* or *PAPERA,* C. amblyrhynchos)
GALAPAGOS SHARK[41]

Color: In this species color is not distinctive. The upper body is medium to dark gray and the underparts white. The fins are plain, except for slightly dusky tips or margins, notably on the caudal, in some individuals.

Morphology: The Galapagos shark possesses a distinct interdorsal ridge; narrow falcate (backswept and curved) pectoral fins; and a first dorsal fin height generally over 11.2% of the total length (this fin is reported to have a relatively stright forward margin, but it has also been noted to vary with maturity). This species is one of the larger members of the genus, perhaps reaching 4 m (13 ft). One specimen was reported measuring 3.7 m (12 ft 1 1/2 in). A length of 3 m (10 ft) is not uncommon.

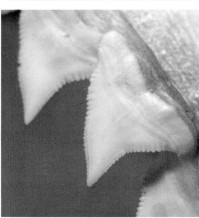

Distribution: This species has a sporadic distribution throughout the warm oceans of the world, but where it occurs, it is often abundant. It is the most abundant inshore shark around islands of the Eastern Tropical Pacific, and it is occasionally found along the Mexican coast. It is found in Hawaii, reported from Rapa in French Polynesia[46], and the author caught one specimen in Rarotonga, Cook Islands. It is also known in the Marshall Islands. In the Indian Ocean, it is only reported

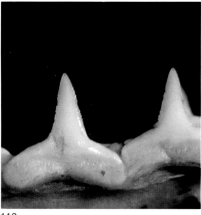

Dentition: $\frac{14 \cdot 1 \cdot 14}{14 \cdot 1 \cdot 14}$ is usual. *Teeth dissimilar in each jaw and uppers broadly triangular and serrate.* **Opposite:** *The Galapagos shark, lacking distinctive coloration, is difficult to identify. In the water only experience in judging body and fin proportions can serve as a guide, e.g., the body is more elongate and the dorsal fin, with straighter leading and trailing edges, is set further back on similar carcharhinids.*

from Walter's Shoal. In the Atlantic it is reported from Bermuda and the Virgin islands.

Habitat: This species is generally an inshore shark found off island drop-offs and banks between 25 and 180 m (80 and 600 ft). It does appear in shallow waters, especially younger individuals which more often range from 2 to 25 m (6 1/2 to 80 ft). Tagging has shown one individual to travel some 50 km (30 mi) over deep water to an adjacent island. Although normally cruising 1 to 3 m (3 to 10 ft) over the bottom, they will approach the surface readily.

Reproduction: The Galapagos shark is thought to mature at over 2 m (6 1/2 feet). A pregnant female was recorded at 2.59 m (8 ft 6 in). In Hawaii litters range from 6 to 16, the normal being 9. The size at birth appears to range between 57 and 80 cm (22 to 32 in).

Feeding: Stomach contents indicate that this species has a decided preference for feeding along the bottom.

Disposition: This species is generally curious and like the gray reef shark can easily be brought to the surface, often in response to the commotion of people or boats. At times, even without feeding stimuli, e.g. speared fish and associated sounds or odors, this species can become quite aggressive, occasionally forcing divers to leave the water. It has been responsible for attacks on man and should be regarded with considerable caution.

CARCHARHINUS LEUCAS
(Valenciennes in Müller & Henle, 1841),
UNKNOWN (probably uncommon in all of Polynesia)
BULL SHARK[4]

Synonyms: Scientifically this species has been known by many names around the world, three of the most notable being *C. zambezensis, C. vanrooyeni* and *C. nicaraguensis.*

Color: This species lacks characteristic coloration, and is a dull gray above and whitish below. In young specimens, under 2.0 m (6 1/2 ft), the fins may be dusky or nearly black tipped.

Morphology: The bull shark lacks an interdorsal ridge; the snout is very short and rounded, and the nostrils have a blunt, triangular lobe on the forward margin. This species reaches 3 m (10 ft).

Distribution: The bull shark is found in warm water of all three major oceans, normally along continents rather than offshore islands. In the Pacific it is found along the coasts of Central and South America. It is also reported from Fiji, and the author recently caught a specimen at Rangiroa Atoll[38]—contrary to the normal distribution. In addition, it occurs in Australia, New Guinea, Asia and Africa, and it is found on both sides of the Atlantic.

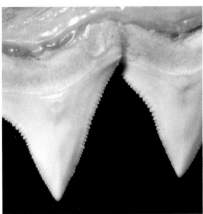

Dentition: $\frac{13\text{-}2\text{-}13}{12\text{-}2\text{-}12}$ *(plus or minus 1 in the lower jaw) is usual. Jaws and teeth large for the size of the shark. Uppers broadly triangular and serrate; lowers uniquely spike-like.* **Opposite**: *The bull shark is a dangerous species perhaps most noted for its penetration and habitation in fresh water. The above specimen was collected from Lake Isabel, San Felipe Guatemala by Dr. Tom Thorsen. Difficult to identify, this species is most readily recognized underwater by its very short, rounded snout generally thick body and lack of characteristic coloration.*

Habitat: The bull shark is commonly found inshore and has a decided preference for turbid, shallow coastal waters in bays and estuaries. It is particularly noted for its penetration, and even habitation, in various rivers and lakes around the world. It is found, although irregularly, in the Atchafalaya Pascagoula river in the Southern U.S., lake Nicaragua in Central America, the Liverpool, Victoria and Swan rivers in Australia, the Ganges and Devi rivers in India, the Karum river—a tributary of the Tigris and Euphrates—in the Persian Gulf, and the Zambezi river in Africa to mention but a few. In lake Nicaragua, it has been shown to swim the 60 mi (100 km) length of the San Juan river, including rapids, separating the lake from the sea[69].

Reproduction: Size at maturity appears to be regional; 2.25 m (7 1/2 ft) is generally the length at onset. Mating and pupping is thought to occur in the summer, June in the Western Atlantic (Northern Hemisphere) and December/January in Africa (Southern Hemisphere). The gestation period is 10 to 12 months, and pups are born at a length of about 75 cm (30 in). The average number varies regionally between 5 and 13.

Feeding: In fresh water the bull shark feeds mainly on bony fish, while in the sea it expresses a preference for other shark, especially the young of the sandbar shark *C. plumbeus*. Off Africa it also feeds commonly on whale, mostly as a consequence of whaling activity in the area. The difference in feeding habits between fresh water and the sea is mainly a matter of availability, for few other shark species penetrate even short distances in fresh water. It may be this lack of normal prey which makes the bull shark so dreaded where it occurs in fresh water, for attacks on man in such areas are not uncommon. The bull shark is also a notable scavenger, and it is noted for the fasting of females during pupping and males during mating.

CARCHARHINUS LIMBATUS
(Valenciennes in Müller & Henle, 1841),
OIHE
BLACKTIP SHARK[4]

Synonyms: Previously known under the scientific name *C. phorcys*, in the Eastern Pacific this species is called the volador.

Color: The upper surface and sides are gray to brown, fading to white below. A band of light coloration penetrates forward on the side of the body from the anal to between the first dorsal and the belly. All fins except the anal are usually tipped black, particularly the underside of the pectorals. However, in many specimens the black tips are so reduced as to be noticeable only upon close observation.

Morphology: This shark lacks the inter-dorsal ridge, has a relatively pointed nose and a steep rise to the back between the snout and first dorsal fin. One of the largest recorded specimens was 2.47 m (8 ft 1 in), indicating a maximum size of around 2.5 m (just over 8 ft).

Distribution: The blacktip is widely distributed in warm waters of all three major oceans. It is found from Baja California to Peru in the Eastern Pacific, and it is known in Hawaii and the Tuamotus. In the Indian Ocean it is widely distributed from Madagascar to the African coast. It is reported on both sides of the Atlantic.

Habitat: The blacktip is generally found inshore, where it commonly inhabits mid-water depths. It can be found along reef drop-offs, but it is also common in turbid lagoon waters. In Africa, it is known to make brief excursions into fresh water.

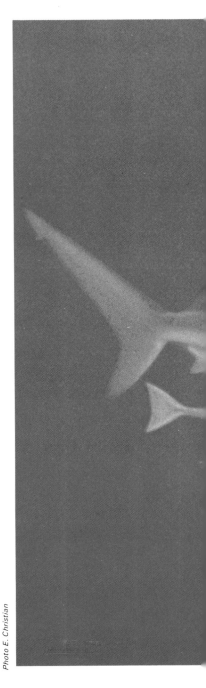

Photo E. Christian

The blacktip, in the Pacific, has reduced black tips on the fins and is best recognized by its pointed snout, high back and a subtle coloration.. This 1964 photo may constitute the first documented occurrence of this species in French Polynesia.

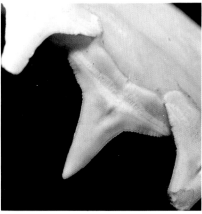

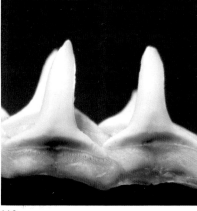

photo D. Nelson

Reproduction: Size at maturity appears to vary regionally between 1.7–1.8 m (5 ft 7 in–5 ft 11 in) off the East coast of Africa, and 1.35–1.50 m (4 ft 5 in –4 ft 11 in) in the Western Atlantic. As the gestation period appears around 12 months, or slightly less, mating and pupping occur about the same time, being November to March off Africa (Southern Hemisphere) and April to January in the Western Atlantic (Northern Hemisphere). In keeping with this hemispherical pattern, the author's data from French Polynesia agrees with the African mating and pupping season. Litters range from 1 to 10 pups, with 5 or 6 being about average. The sex ratio is probably 1:1 but data indicate a slightly higher percentage of

Dentition: $\frac{15-2 \text{ or } 3-15}{15-1-15}$. Upper and lower teeth dissimilar, but uppers more spike-like than usual indicating a holding emphasis. **Top and Right**: Although often shy, the blacktip becomes quite brazen under stimulated conditions as in this case when trash fish were discarded from the warf at Avatoru, Rangiroa while sorting fish for export to Tahiti (16 mm sequence).

males are produced. Pups are born at about 60 cm (24 in) of length.

Activity: Telemetry tagging investigations at Rangiroa Atoll indicated a tidal rhythm, with individuals remaining in turbid lagoon water most of the time and traveling to the pass and nearby outer reefs during low slack.

Feeding: The high percentage of bony fish and the presence of several fast swimming species in stomach contents indicates the blacktip is a capable, active predator which spends much of its time mid-water, although it does feed off the bottom on occasion. In Rangiroa, this shark is among the several species which is noted picking up discarded trash fish when interisland freighters are loading fish for export to Tahiti. The blacktip, more commonly than the other species, jets the discarded fish before they reach the bottom. The fact that this species is one of the few noted to have a body temperature greater (1.2° C— 2.16° F) than the surrounding water would support its rapid swimming ability, and the holding emphasis of the teeth would seem well-suited to catching fish on the run.

Disposition: This species is generally shy or indifferent under unstimulated conditions. Under such circumstances it is unlikely to bother swimmers or divers. However, when spearfishing, especially in turbid water, it can become very aggressive. This species was responsible for a non-fatal attack in Rangiroa under similar conditions[39]. In clear water this species is usually more reserved, seldom approaching closer than 15 m (50 ft) after which it normally departs rapidly. On one occasion while baiting in clear water on an outer reef, the author observed several small gray reef sharks and blackfin reef sharks attempting to eat the head of a large fish. A blacktip was observed, but it would only approach the bait when the observer on the surface moved away. It eventually moved in to take the head with the smaller sharks scurring behind as it rapidly departed.

CARCHARHINUS LONGIMANUS

(Poey, 1861),

MAO PARATA

OCEANIC WHITETIP SHARK[4]

Synonyms: Formerly known under the scientific name *Pterolamiops magnipinnis,* it is likely that the present name may be changed to *C. maou* in the future, pending the results of a revision of the genus.

Color: The body is generally grayish with an occasional brownish cast fading, not necessarily evenly, to a dirty white below. Tips of the first dorsal, pectorals, pelvics and tail fin are white, but the gradation between the white tipped fins and the basic body color is mediated via shades of irregular mottling. The ventral surface of the pelvics, the anal and the tip of the second dorsal are either dusky or black tipped. Dark blotches or saddles are usually visible in front of the second dorsal and tail origins and are sometimes visible just aft of the second dorsal base. A series of small, indistinct dark blotches may be seen in the interdorsal area. Embryos have distinct black tipped fins which it would seem might linger to a certain degree in smaller specimens.

Morphology: The oceanic whitetip possesses a characteristic dorsal fin shape which is high and broadly rounded. The pectorals are very long and also rounded at the tips. The interdorsal ridge, normally prominent, is reported lacking in some individuals. One of the largest reported specimens of this species was recorded at 3.5 m (11 ft 5 3/4 in), and it is said they may grow longer. However, specimens over 3 m (10 ft) are by far the exception.

Distribution: The oceanic whitetip is

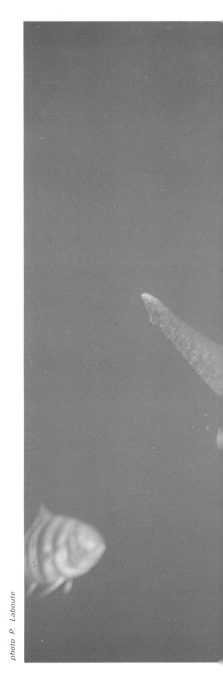

photo P. Laboute

The oceanic whitetip, commonly escorted by a squadron of pilot fish, Naucrates ductor, *has characteristic white tipped fins and a distinctly shaped dorsal.*

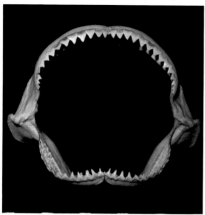

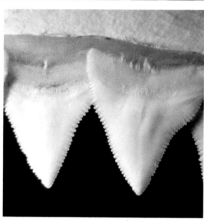

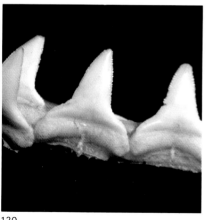

widely distributed throughout the warm waters of the Atlantic, Indian and Pacific Oceans. In the Central Pacific this species is found between 20° North and South. They appear most commonly in water above 21° C (69.8° F) but have occurred in water as cool as 15° C (59° F). It has been speculated that owing to the wide distribution over vast areas of the sea, this species is one of the most abundant larger animals on earth.

Habitat: This species, as the name implies, expresses a definite preference for the pelagic environment, generally not being found in water less than about 185 m (600 ft). It occasionally comes inshore, especially around oceanic islands with sharp drop offs. At Rangiroa Atoll, on at least 3 occasions, they have been observed over the outer reef in 20 m (65 ft) or less of water, and the author fished one in about the same depth off Rarotonga in the Cook Islands.

Reproduction: The oceanic whitetip matures at under 2 m (6 1/2 ft), with females apparently maturing at a smaller size than males (the reverse of most carcharhinids) ; although, as in most members of the genus, females obtain the largest size. Breeding and pupping appears to occur in May and June, and the gestation period is about 12 months. Litters range to 15, but 5 to 8 is the normal. Larger females appear to produce larger litters. Pups are thought born at about 65 cm (25 1/2 in); however, as free swimming individuals less than 80 to 90 cm (31 1/2 to 35 1/2 in) have not been

Dentition: $\frac{14 \cdot 2 \cdot 14}{14 \cdot 2 \cdot 14}$ is normal. *Teeth in each jaw dissimilar and uppers broadly triangular and serrated.* **Opposite**: *A near full term oceanic whitetip embryo possesses a reverse color pattern with fins tipped black. As the new born of this species are unknown, it is not known when the fin tips turn white.*

found, either pups are larger at birth or the pupping and rearing grounds are unknown. The latter is believed to be the case.

Feeding: One study shows the major items in the stomach of the oceanic whitetip are squids of various species (52 %), bony fish (35 %) and whale meat—resulting from whaling activities (9 %). Among the bony fish are tuna and dolphin, perhaps indicating that this species is capable of capturing fast swimmers. One report indicated that they follow schools of tuna and take advantage of the tuna's preoccupation when feeding on small fish to attack[3]. Other reports[44] cite observations of this species swimming through feeding schools of tuna with their mouths wide open, concluding that they merely depended on chance for either the tuna or the bait fish to literally swim into their open mouths. As this behavior was displayed by numerous individuals, it appeared a fixed behavior pattern indicating a common method of feeding. Another observation reported[44] an oceanic whitetip feeding on a tight school of bait fish in a casual but different manner. It repeatedly, approached the school, which appeared oblivious to the sharks activity, taking bites out of the perifery in a fashion reminiscent of taking bites out of an apple. These sharks are also scavengers. The author caught one with a bait made of a plastic sack filled with well cleaned chicken bones, and the specimen caught in Rarotonga contained 3 chicken heads, 2 slabs of butchered meat, 1—38 cm (15 in) diameter leaf and 1—48 cm (19 in) pine needle.

Disposition: The oceanic whitetip is generally brazen and sometimes outright aggressive. Although occasionally just circling widely and departing, this species may also move in very close, even to the point of contact, sometimes bumping objects or divers. The oceanic whitetip is difficult to deter, sometimes returning repeatedly even after blows as solid as that of a well directed oar. Their casualness should not be misinterpreted, for as in natural feeding, they may take a bite without appearing at all excited. This species has attacked man.

CARCHARHINUS MELANOPTERUS
(Quoy & Gaimard, 1824)
MAURI
BLACKFIN REEF SHARK[10]

Synonyms: Due to its widespread and common occurrence this shark has many local names: *ootea* (Leeward Society Islands), *vaki* (Tuamotu), *mano* (Marquesas)[3] and *mango tea* (Cook Islands)[72]. It is widely known as the blacktip reef shark[41], but the above common name, also widely used[10] avoids confusion with the blacktip shark, *C. limbatus.*

Color: The basic body color of this species is beige or brownish, with a light band penetrating forward from the anal fin to just between the first dorsal and belly. Its most characteristic markings, by which it can be identified immediately, are the prominent black tips on all fins. On the first dorsal, the black tip is accentuated in most specimens by an underlying band of light pigmentation, separating it from the basic body color. On the tail the trailing edge is black with a precise demarcation between this black pigmentation and the basic body color. The tail is also accentuated by lighter pigmentation forward, especially preceding the entirely black lower lobe.

Morphology: The blackfin reef shark lacks an interdorsal ridge and has a blunt, rounded snout. It is relatively small, probably not even reaching 2m (6 1/2 ft). One of the largest recorded was 1.8 m (5 ft 11 in), but most are less than 1.6 m (5 ft 3 in).

Distribution: The blackfin reef shark is widespread throughout the Indo-Pacific region. It is common to continents and oceanic islands,

One of the handsomest of sharks, the blackfin reef shark—alias blacktip reef shark—is instantly recognizable by characteristic black tipped and fringed finnage.

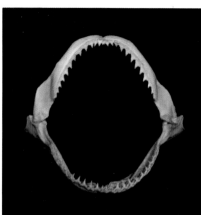

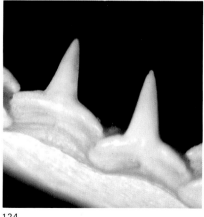

being noted in the Hawaiian, French Polynesian, Cook, Marshall and Mariana Islands to mention but a few. It is known in the South from Australia, North from Japan and Westward to the coast of Africa. It may extend via the Suez Canal into the Mediterranean. It is absent in the Eastern Pacific and, also, for no apparent reason, at certain oceanic islands including: Johnston, Marcus and Rarotonga[72]. It is one of the 3 most abundant species in French Polynesia. Although once common in Hawaii, it is now less abundant.

Habitat: The blackfin reef shark exhibits a decided preference for shallow[30] and generally clearer water. It is most frequently found in 3 m (10 ft) or less of water, often on reef flats so shallow that the dorsal fin is exposed. Smaller individuals, especially, are found in such shallow water, while adults occur deeper, sometimes near to and over reef drop-offs but probably not much beyond.

Reproduction: This species matures at just over a meter (39 in) in length. One of the smallest pregnant females recorded measured 1.12 m (3 ft 8 in) and one of the smallest mature males 1.09 m (3 ft 4 in). Breeding data are scanty[60]. One report indicates that in the Indian Ocean there are 2 seasons between June/July and December/January. In French Polynesia evidence supports this dual pattern. Gestation is reported as possibly 16 months. Pups generally number 4 or less per

Dentition: $\frac{12 \cdot 1 \text{ or } 2 \cdot 12}{11 \quad -1- \quad 11}$ is normal. *Adult males have more sharply curved cusps along the outer edge than females. Teeth are otherwise very similar to those of the gray reef shark.*
Opposite: *Although normally timid, when baited the backfin reef shark is a persistent and capable shark. Under such conditions it can sometimes be very closely approached, and is usually not dangerous.*

litter, ranging from 40 to 50 cm (15 to 20 in) at birth, but evidence indicates a regional diversity. Central Pacific specimens are known to be born at less than 33 cm (13 in).

Activity: Telemetry tagging data at Rangiroa Atoll indicated a high continuous rate of activity accentuated at night, while conventional tagging indicated that some individuals remained in the same general area for long periods of time—at least two years.

Feeding: The blackfin reef shark is basically a shallow water predator and scavenger which feeds mostly on bony fish and, to a lesser degree, on octopus. One specimen had parts of another shark in its stomach. When attacking bait they are fast and aggressive. The author witnessed a rare incident of natural predation in which a small surgeon fish was selected from among several feeding in about 3 m (10 ft) of water over open, sloping sand. The shark pursued rapidly, as the fish, being no match for speed, darted erratically from side to side. Not losing the shark along the bottom, the fish headed in a similar fashion toward the surface. After a 10 m (about 30 ft) chase to within a meter (about 3 ft) of the surface, the shark caught the fish, and ingested it whole in a single quick gulp.

Disposition: Normally the blackfin reef shark is easily frightened. Under unstimulated conditions it usually flees at the sight of a diver. Even when baited, it will depart if the diver moves closer, usually to return a minute or so later trying to find a more opportune moment to get the bait. Occasionally loners are met which deviate from this general pattern, sometimes departing from the bottom and pestering divers mid-water or at the surface. In shallow water or when encountered in numbers, this species can become aggressive, and there are a few attacks on record, some involving mistaken identity and most of them involving persons wading on reef flats[60]. An unusual attack occurred in the Cook Islands in which a pearl diver was bitten on the foot just after leaving the bottom at about 20 m (65 ft)[72].

125

GALEOCERDO CUVIER
(Peron & Lesueur, 1822)
MAO TORE TORE
TIGER SHARK[4][41]

Synonyms: New spelling supercedes *G. cuvieri.* The tiger shark is a notable species, and therefore has several local names: *mao taita* and *ruhia* (Tuamotus) *maio* and *mano vakovako* (Marquesas) and *mango* (Gambiers)[3].

Color: The name of this species is derived from its color pattern. From the embryo to adolescence or early adulthood, the tiger shark possesses a pattern of dark stripes or transverse bands, which gradually lessen as the shark matures giving way to a mottled dull gray. The underside is white, but the change is usually abrupt and irregular with white invading the basic body color along the margin.

Morphology: The tiger shark possesses a distinct caudal keel, has a very blunt, squared-off snout and a distinctly pointed upper lobe on the tail. They are thought to reach or exceed 6 m (20 ft), but the largest recorded is in the 5.5 m (18 ft) range. The commonest adult size is between 3 and 4.25 m (10 and 14 ft), 114 to 455 kg (250 to 1,000 lbs).

Distribution: This species is quite common in all the warm oceans of the world, occurring almost everywhere within warm temperate to tropical waters.

Habitat: The tiger shark is basically an inshore species, but one which is not uncommonly found at sea. It generally seems to prefer turbid areas around continents, extensive island masses or high volcanic islands where fresh water run off may be heavy (a source of food) and where currents

The tiger shark, named for its stripped pattern at birth, fades to a mottled dull gray in older adults.

126

are not so strong[71]. However, the tiger shark is at times, relatively abundant in other areas, e.g., around atolls or in larger and deeper atoll lagoons.

Reproduction: The tiger shark is reported to mature at over 2.9 m (9 1/2 ft). Pupping occurs in April to June (Northern Hemisphere). The autor's data for French Polynesia suggests November to January pupping (Southern Hemisphere) as all gravid females examined during April to June contained mid-term embryos. The tiger shark produces large litters, numbering up to 80 or more pups, thought to be about 51 to 76 cm (20 to 30 in) at birth.

Activity: The tiger shark appears to be nocturnal. At night they commonly enter bays, estuaries, passes and lagoons not frequented by day, and at these times they may be found in water so shallow they can hardly swim. By day they remain deeper, e.g., in sufficiently deep lagoons and off outer reefs, making encounters with the tiger shark rare for divers or even spearfishermen. It appears some individuals, basically adults, become semi-resident around oceanic islands, ranging their perimeter or a portion thereof. These trends are shown by fishing data[67] which additionally indicate that once a semi-resident population is removed, it is replaced gradually by smaller, possibly pelagic, individuals moving into the area. Such residency is not inclusive to all individuals, for tagging has shown some to move hundreds of kilometers (miles)[59].

Feeding: Perhaps no animal on earth, the goat included, is more notorious for its diversified diet. This probably accounts for the tiger shark's habitat preference near rivers and harbors which provide refuse. The tiger shark is described as feeding upon anything sufficiently small to enter its cavernous mouth, including innumerable inedible items. It is also a capable predator, and one which feeds not uncommonly on other shark (10% of stomach contents)[67] [71], including flesh of its own kind. It is noted to feed commonly on rays (leopard and manta), occasionally on bony fish and to a lesser degree on mammals (seals and porpoises), turtles, sea snakes and sea birds. Surprisingly, it has been noted to gorge itself on occasion with lobster, conch and sand crabs (Limulus). Although normally swimming at a graceful pace, when stimulated, the tiger shark is capable of rapid bursts of speed and tremendous power.

Disposition: The tiger shark is second only to the white shark in recorded and authenticated attacks on man[7]— some attacks even including multiple victims in the same encounter. It is commonly noted to attack boats. One account states that although native spearfishermen frequently continue their activity amongst even a dozen or so sharks of several other species, they depart in haste on the rare occasion in which a tiger shark is seen[3]. The author has observed several free swimming specimens during daylight hours which were attracted to other tigers hooked during the preceding evening. On several occasions they were observed from within the water at the edge of a boat, with periodic test dives ventured toward them as they passed beneath or departed. During these test dives they occasionally turned back on the observer. Although their interest in the diver was reserved, they expressed

---

A freed mid-term tiger shark decends in gossamer veils of embryonic tissue.

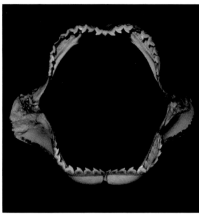

no reluctance or fear and, therefore were regarded as too dangerous to chance close encounters. Although several people have seen the tiger underwater (some at night) and survived, many have not. Divers have witnessed a tiger shark swim away with their partner in its mouth never to be seen again. One person reported that a shaft from a speargun elicited a hasty departure by an adult attracted during blue water spear fishing.

Having the ability to breathe without forward movement for considerable lenghts of time[33], the tiger shark usually remains alive once caught. The author has dived with many such specimens and found them to swim obliviously in continuous circles about the buoy to which the line was attached. Occasionally they would change direction or even hang vertically on the hook showing no sign of life for brief periods of time. Under such conditions they can normally be approached from any direction, and are reluctant to alter their course until touched, at which time they initiate a brief burst of speed, followed by renewed circular swimming. However, a freshly hooked shark may be considerably more active, and other persons having fished tiger sharks report that some will even attack the boat.

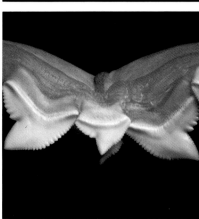

Dentition: $\frac{11 \cdot 1 \cdot 11}{11 \cdot 1 \cdot 11}$ is usual. Teeth in both jaws alike, of distinctive shape, and large even for such big sharks. The single medium tooth may be oblique to either side of center, resulting in right or left toothed sharks.
Opposite, top: A hooked and fatigued tiger, transformed from a powerful predator into passive giant. **Below right:** A reef whitetip was good bait for this tiger shark's capture. **Below left:** collection for science.

NEGAPRION ACUTIDENS
(Rüppell, 1835)
ARAVA
SOUTH PACIFIC LEMON SHARK

Synonyms: The taxonomic status of this genus is most uncertain. It may be represented by one world-wide species or several, which could eventually result in most being synonomyzed.

Color: The upper body is usually brownish to beige, often with a yellowish tinge which fades below to a yellowish, off-white.

Morphology: This species is characterized by its large second dorsal. The first dorsal is placed about midway between the pectoral and pelvic fins. The pectoral fins are falcate (recurved backward). This shark approaches 3 m (10 ft) and is reasonably heavy bodied.

Distribution: Due to the taxonomic confusion of the genus, distribution is difficult to define. A lemon shark, *N. brevirostris,* occurs in the Western Atlantic from Massachusetts in the U.S. to the Amazon in Brasil. Another, *N. fronto,* is known in the Eastern Pacific from Peru, *N. acutidens* occurs in French Polynesia, another species in the Marshall islands and *N. queenslandicus* is reported from Australia.

Habitat: Lemon sharks are decidely inshore species, inhabiting bays and estuaries. In French Polynesia, *N. acutidens* occurs on the outer reefs and in the lagoons. This species is very much bottom oriented but will approach the surface if stimulated. It is commonly found ranging along the bottom, on the reef shelf in less than 30 m (100 ft) of water. It also is abundant inside lagoons, often in, but not restricted to turbid, still water away from passes. The young are found in very shallow water of less than one meter (39 in) on reef flats, often with

The South Pacific lemon shark is easily identified by the second dorsal being nearly as largas the first dorsal fin, which is set well forwar

their dorsal fins out of the wate Reports of this species, *N. acutidens* pursuing fishing boats at sea, raisin havock with tuna catches[3], ar probably erroneous.

Reproduction: *N. brevirostris* mature at a length of over 2.25 m (7 ft 4 1/ in). Mating is reported, in the Norther hemisphere, a few months prior to an following May, which appears to b the peak. As the gestation period i between 10 and 12 months, matin and pupping occur about the sam time of year. Litters range from 5 t 18 each, 11 being about norma Pups are born at a length of aroun

50 cm (24 in). The author's data for *N. acutidens* in Rangiroa Atoll (Southern Hemisphere) shows May embryos are mid-term indicating a December/January pupping season in the Southern Hemisphere. These data also indicate, that pups range in number from one to eleven and are likely to be smaller at birth, based on free swimming individuals observed in the lagoon estimated to be about 45 cm (18 in) in length.

Feeding: Stomach contents include bottom dwelling fish and rays, confirming the inshore, bottom dwelling habits of this species.

Disposition: The arava, *N. acutidens*, is generally shy even when baited. The author has observed, time and again, the reluctance of large individuals to approach divers, usually departing from the area after briefly being seen at the limits of visibility. On one occasion, a 10 kg (22 lb) grouper was placed on the bottom in 10 m (33 ft) of water, and an adult arava was attracted. This shark fled upon the slightest movement of the observers, and only succeeded in grabbing the bait in a quick run after numerous arrivals and departures over a 30 minute period. On other occasions, this species would not take the bait at all unless the divers departed from the water, indicating that such reluctance is a general species pattern. However, in shallow water, young individuals of about 1 m (3 ft) are often noted to be most aggressive. The author and his wife were almost

133

photo T. Sciarotta

bitten in 30 cm (12 in) of water by an approximately 1 m (39 in) individual which made repeated passes prior to and after being shot at with a speargun. It eventually departed for unknown reasons—in a wild dash across the reef

flat, breaching the surface in its haste.

The arava is widely noted for its malevolence if disturbed. Attempting to touch, let alone prodding, shooting at or spearing, is reported to result

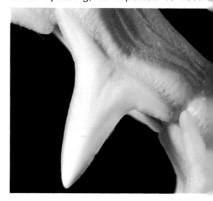

n an attack released in anger against the person or boat involved. It is even reported that an enraged arava will circle a coral head upon which its tormentor has sought refuge, waiting for hours before departing[3]. Moreover,

there have been incidents where the arava adopted this attack behavior in which the victim was unaware of having done anything to provoke the shark[1]. This behavior, perhaps to a lesser degree, has been noted in *N. brevirostris,* which is known to have attacked man and boats. Because of their apparently similar behavior and the more than substantial size and dentition, the arava should be treated with respect.

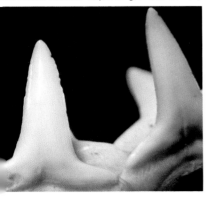

The author surfacing with a South Pacific lemon shark collected at Rangiroa Atoll. This species, although usually timid and difficult to approach, has a paradoxically unsavory reputation. **Dentition:** $\frac{14\text{-}4\text{-}14}{12\text{-}3\text{-}12}$ *is the count from the above shark. Teeth in each jaw similar but not precisely identical. Their spike-like shape indicates a holding emphasis.*

TRIAENODON OBESUS
(Rüppell, 1835)
MAMARU
REEF WHITETIP SHARK[41]

Synonyms: Also known as *torire* (Tuamotu), *peata* (Marquesas)[3] and *maru* (Cook Islands)[72].

Color: The reef whitetip has a basic body color of darkish gray above, often with a few definite, randomly spaced, dark spots commonly 1 or 2 cm (3/8 to 3/4in) in diameter. This color fades to white below. The most characteristic features of color are conspicuous whitetips on the first dorsal and at least the upper lobe of the tail.

Morphology: The reef whitetip has a large second dorsal, conspicuous ridges over the eyes, flattened head, blunt snout and prominent nasal flaps. It is reported to reach 2.2 m (7ft 3in). However, this is very large, as few individuals exceed or even reach 1.7 m (5ft 7in).

Distribution: This species is found throughout the warm waters of the Pacific and Indian Oceans. It is common around the Galapagos and Cocos Islands but rare along the continental coast in the Eastern-Pacific. It occurs in Hawaii, French Polynesia, Cook and Marshall Islands, to mention but a few areas in the Central Pacific, and it is known in Australia. In French Polynesia it is one of the three most abundant species.

Habitat: This species expresses a preference for reefs around atolls and lagoons. As it is capable of respiring in the absence of currents or forward motion, it is often seen at rest on the sand. It is decidely bottom oriented and takes refuge in crevices and caves. It almost never approaches the sur-

The reef whitetip is distinguished by white tips on the dorsals and tail fin and a somewhat atypical body form.

136

face, except perhaps in shallow water, and it is most common at depths between 10 and 20 m (30 and 60ft).

Reproduction: A pregnant female was collected with two well developed but less than full term pups at Rangiroa Atoll in the month of May. Also in May at Aratura Atoll, four free swimming specimens found under the same coral head were taken which measured between 64 and 76 cm (25 and 30in). Three of these specimens possessed notable umbilical scars.

At Rangiroa, on August 21, 1977, a captive 141 cm (4ft 8in) reef whitetip gave birth to 3 female pups ranging 55 to 60 cm (21½ to 23½in) in length. If pupping is seasonal, these data may indicate a Fall/Winter season in the Tuamotus (Southern Hemisphere). Litters appear small, averaging around 3 pups born at a length near 60 cm (2ft).

Activity: Telemetry and conventional tagging studies[54] indicate that these sharks possess both a nocturnal and tidal rhythm, being most active in darkness and during slack tides (where currents are prevalent). They commonly remain within the refuge of the same caves by day, often in association with other individuals. Their preference for a given cave periodically changes. Previous inhabitants generally vacate the old cave and find new associations with other individuals in another cave. They are quite resident and remain in a rather restricted area for months and in some cases years. Eventually they seem to give up one area and move to to another, becoming vagabonds for the period in between. Although relatively inactive by day (less so at slack

Reef whitetips aggregated during baiting to record tagged individuals and tag unmarked sharks.

water when tidal currents are prevalent), they learn to associate the sound of local spearfishermen with the frequent occurrence of wounded fish which are easy prey. In areas where such spearfishing activity is routine, even the dropping of an anchor or the firing of a speargun may bring these sharks from their caves in anticipation of an easy meal.

Feeding: The reef whitetip shark excells in feeding on the bottom and especially among cracks and crevices. The diet consists of small fish and notably octopus, both of which are probably most frequently captured at night. It is attracted to sounds and follows odors well, but its vision appears wanting at times, as it frequently passes over bait having to circle to find it. If a wounded fish

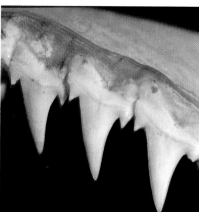

Dentition: $\frac{19\text{-}5\text{-}19}{20\text{-}5\text{-}20}$ *appears common. Teeth small, uniquely tricuspid, alike in each jaw and best suited to holding.* **Below:** *A reef whitetip demonstrating its ability to feed in a confined space on the bottom.* **Opposite:** *Miss Gwen Cornfield, at the author's request, hand feeding a reef whitetip shark off the end of a pole spear to graphically illustrate "shark* *sense" (see p. 72)* *whereby specific knowledge of a given species and its behavior results in a predictable situation.*

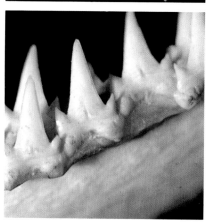

escapes into a crevice, these sharks may, independently or in a group, jam themselves into an opening to get at the prey. If they fail to get the fish immediately, after a brief struggle, they may rest momentarily looking like so many dead sharks stuffed into a hole. But such a method of feeding is the whitetip's forte, and eventually one will find the prey. When it gets a hold, if the prey is too large to swallow, it shakes and thrashes its body in an attempt to obtain leverage enough to remove a bite with its poor cutting teeth. In this endeavor they sometimes topple coral heads and otherwise tear up the reef, apparently oblivious to the bruising and abrasion of their bodies. Such observations of feeding behavior are not entirely uncommon, but they are the exception, as the reef whitetip usually locates and dispenses with its prey in short order.

Disposition: Under unstimulated conditions this species is perhaps best described as indifferent, for it is neither attracted to nor particularly repelled by divers unless pursued, at which time it will usually depart or remain at a distance. Under stimulated conditions. e.g., during spearfishing, it is easily attracted and will actively seek the source of an attractant stimulus so long as its location is not far off the bottom. The author has hand fed these sharks under otherwise natural conditions. The reef whitetip shark will sometimes approach a diver closely, but it only very rarely show signs of aggressiveness. On those uncommon occasions where divers have been bitten by this species, it seems likely that the majority were accidents, where the shark did not have intentions of biting upon original contact and only did so defensively afterward. However, there is one account where a diver felt his defensive maneuver of bracing a speargun on his hip as the shark made contact with the spear tip, was all that saved him from becoming the victim of a directed attack[32].

LAMNIDAE

ISURUS OXYRINCHUS
(Rafinesque, 1810)
MAO AAHI
MAKO OR SHORT-FINNED MAKO SHARK[4][21]

photo J. Garrick

Synonyms: This genus, having undergone a revision,[21] has been found to possess only two species, the other being the long-finned mako, *I. paucus*. Therefore, all other previous names are synomized, the most familiar having been *I. glaucus*. Regarding local names this shark is called *parata* (Marquesas) and *para mango* (Cook Islands).

Color: The upper body of this species is a deep blue, gradually fading to pure white below.

Morphology: The short-finned mako is characterized by a conical snout; very long gill slits, all of about equal length; pectoral fin length about 70% of the snout to pectoral origin distance; a caudal keel; and a tail fin with upper lobe only slightly larger than the lower. It reaches at least 3.66 m (12ft) and 455 kg (1,000lbs), but 1.5 to 2.5 m (5 to 8ft) is more common.

Distribution: This shark is world-wide in temperate and tropical seas within its preferred temperature range of around 18.5°C (65°F).

Habitat: The short-finned mako is basically a pelagic species, but it is occasionally found inshore, normally adjacent to deep water. Due to its cooler temperature preference, this species is usually found deep in the tropics. It is said to be common around Tahiti at a depth of 200 to 400 m (650 to 1,300ft), and it is occasionally taken in this area by marlin fishermen while trolling artificial lures just under the surface.

Reproduction: Information is scanty, but litters are thought to average about 10 pups of around 51 cm

Dentition: $\frac{10\text{-}14}{10\text{-}15}$ on each side of jaws account. for the wide variation. Teeth are alike in eac. jaw, unserrate and very elongate indicating holding emphasis.

(20in) length.

Feeding: This species generally feeds on mackerel, herring, tuna and simila smaller fish. However, larger individuals not uncommonly feed on porpoise and even swordfish.

Disposition: Even encountered unde unstimulated conditions this species is frightening, for its pace is fast However, under such conditions it is not likely to be encountered no intently interested in a diver.

photo J. Garrick

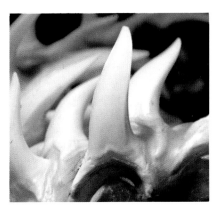

Top: The mako is fast and powerful due to enlarged gill-respiratory apparatus, nearly symmetrical tail fin, supporting caudal keel and a blood, heat exchange mechanism providing a degree of warm bloodedness.

Under feeding stimulated conditions makos may make repeated fast and close passes usually veering off at the last moment[18].

If the source of the attractant stimuli is not readily determinable, e.g., as is sometimes the case with odors, it may come up the odor corridor, rapidly dashing to any small visible objects.

A recent observation of peculiar swimming seems potentially related to display behavior[46], which would indicate a forewarning may exist in this species prior to non-feeding motivated attacks, and there are indications this species may attack for such reasons[58]. This peculiar behavior was described as porpoising followed by rapid "figure eight" swimming. It appears that the supporting caudal keel permits almost instantaneous and reversible vertical movements in the water facilitating the above behavior.

In any event, the mako has attacked man, and it is to be considered dangerous. Its speed and attendant behavior will command the respect of anyone encountering it in the water.

143

ORECTOLOBIDAE

NEBRIUS CONCOLOR
(Rüppell, 1835)
MAO ROHOI
INDO-PACIFIC NURSE SHARK

Synonyms: The most recent is *Ginglymostoma ferrugineum*. *G. brevicaudatum* sometimes listed as a synonym is actually a recognized species of the Indian Ocean fauna which reaches a length of about 1 m (39in). Local synonyms include *nohipiri* or *mohi piri* in the Tuamotus. Another common name for this species is sleeping shark, which is confusing as other species are sometimes referred to by the same name.

Color: This species possesses a basic brown coloration which varies from beige to shades of gray. Due to color differences, locals often considered them as two species. However, the author maintained a beige specimen for several days in 10 m (about 30ft) of water on a white sand bottom in full sun. This shark developed thousands of tiny black pigment spots rendering a darker coloration tending towards gray. It would, therefore, appear that those which spend their days in caves are light in color while those which remain in full exposure become "suntanned" or darker. This basic coloration fades gradually to creamy white beneath.

Morphology: This species is easily recognizable even at a distance by the presence of the first dorsal fin set far back over the pelvic fins. It has a large second dorsal set just behind, and the tail fin almost lacks the lower lobe, giving it the impression of substantial length. Upon close inspection a fleshy barbel will be found in front of each nostril. This species is common to 2 m (6 1/2ft) and may reach 2.5 to 3 m (8 to 10ft).

Distribution: This species is found in

warm waters from the Red Sea and Australia to the islands of French Polynesia. It is not reported from Hawaii, is uncommon around Tahiti and its presence in the Tuamotu varies.

Habitat: This species is a bottom dwelling, inshore shark found in both lagoons and along outer reefs. Generally it prefers coral reefs or rugged terrain providing shelter. Where

uch refuge is not available, this spe-
ies may be found lying relatively
xposed in a depression or crevice.

is not uncommon to find this shark
n water so shallow that the dorsal
ns break the surface.

eproduction: This species gives birth
o living young. The size and number
f young is probably similar to its
astern Pacific and Atlantic relative,
. cirratum, which produces 20 to

*The Indo-Pacific nurse shark is characterized
by the nearly like sized dorsals placed close
together and set far back.*

30, 30 cm (12in) pups.

Activity: The Indo-Pacific nurse shark
is primarily nocturnal, but a few
individuals have been observed to
leave their day-time refuge in caves
or crevices. During the day they are
quite sluggish and disposed to what
appears to be nearly continuous slum-

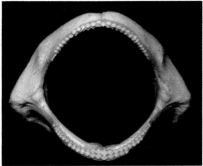

Top, right: *The Indo-Pacific nurse shark, also characterized by barbels visible in front of each nostril, is only rarely active by day.* **Top, left**: *Individuals habitually seeking shelter by day, e.g., caves and crevices, are light in color. At Manihi Atoll such a specimen, placed in the village pond, "suntanned" to the deep brown of its gregarious pool mates within several weeks of daily exposure to the sun.* **Dentition** $\frac{12 \cdot 1 \cdot 12}{12 \cdot 1 \cdot 12}$ *is usual. Teeth alike in both jaws and adapted to the crushing and grinding of crustaceans and molluscs.*

ber. They are gregarious, and several individuals are sometimes found together, often piled in random fashion across or on top of each other. By night they become active, and can be found slowly foraging on the reef

moving in and out of the coral.

Feeding: This species has powerful jaws, albeit small for their size. The dentition is suited to both crushing and holding but not particularly to cutting. Their diet consists mainly of whatever they can find including sea urchins, crabs, octopus, squid, and, on occasion, small fish. Nurse sharks frequently feed by placing their mouth in the closest possible proximity to a prey being sensed in crevices, opening the mouth with a vacuum substantial enough to suck the prey from the safty of its refuge. Studies indicate that the suction created is substantial, and this behavior is easily observed when feeding captive indi-viduals small pieces of fish which fall just out of reach.

Disposition: This particular species, by contrast to *G. cirratum* and many other Orectolobids, is unusually docile. At Manihi atoll in the Tua-motus[3], several individuals are kept in an enclosure and local children frequently ride or play with these sharks. However, even this species can become defensive, if not aggres-ive, and one day a child was bitten. A bite by this species is brutal for, as is true of the entire family, they are reluctant to release the victim. On one occasion a nurse shark had to be killed and the jaws pried open before the victim could be freed.

147

RHINCODONTIDAE

RHINCODON TYPUS
(Smith, 1825)
UNKNOWN
WHALE SHARK[4]

Synonyms: An alternate spelling is Rhiniodontidae and *Rhiniodon typus.*

Color: The whale shark has a dark basic body color above, with a reddish or greenish brown cast which has superimposed over it a characteristic pattern of alternating vertical bands of white or yellowish spots and stripes.

Morphology: The body has several (usually three to each side) longitudinal ridges running obliquely from above the gill slits downward to above the pelvics. The mouth is terminal, at the end of the snout area; eyes small; and gill slits large. This shark is reported to attain a length of 18 m (59ft) and a weight of 41,000 kg (90,000lbs)[47].

Dentition: The whale shark possesses some 3,000 small teeth throught to be of little, if any, value in feeding.

Distribution: This species is known in almost all tropical and occasionally cooler waters of the world. Although it is nowhere abundant, it is perhaps most common in the Indian Ocean off Mauritius and the Seychelles. It has been sighted not infrequently in French Polynesia, notably between Moorea, Tetiaroa and Tahiti.

Habitat: The whale shark is generally pelagic, although it is occasionally found close to shore and even in atoll lagoons, including Tikehou and Rangiroa in the Tuamotus.

Reproduction: Little is known of this species except that it is an egg layer. An egg, the world's largest[47], measuring 30 cm × 14 cm × 8 cm (12in × 5.5in × 3.1in) and containing an embryo apparently close to hatching, was trawled up from a depth of 57 m

photo E. Gould

(187ft) in the Gulf of Mexico. Th embryo very closely resembled a adult in form and color.

Feeding: The whale shark possesses spongy tissue between the gill arche which filters water passing through th gill openings. Anything not passin through is consumed which, in additio to various planktonic forms, include small bait fish and occasionally eve tuna. The inclusion of tuna is base upon observations of a unique feedin behavior. On one occasion a whal shark was observed feeding verticall in the water where it moved rhythmi cally up and down with its mouth ope and head emerging periodically. A its head cleared the surface, wate passed through the gill openings straining the contents. On anothe

occasion several individuals, dispersed widely in the same general area, were observed simultaneously feeding in this manner among bait fish. It was noted that these fish, and also tuna feeding upon them, were captured in this manner. The tuna, in their frenzied feeding on the bait fish, would apparently leap right into the open mouth of the whale shark, and although some again leaped out, it was thought that many were eaten.

Disposition: The whale shark is usually completely indifferent toward divers, permitting them to approach and even hitchhike on the dorsal fin. If annoyed they usually sink below or move out of reach by gradually increasing their speed. Some even seem to enjoy the treatment, returning for

Above and following page: *The whale shark, largest fish on earth, is a gigantic polkadotted clown which tolerates or even welcomes the close attention of divers.*

seconds. However, a note of caution: a pair of boots was found in the stomach of one of these creatures, which casts suspicion upon the complete harmlessness of the species. Moreover, there are several incidents recorded indicating aggressiveness. Off Mauritius three boats were attacked in one year, in one case spinning a power boat in the 6 m (20ft) range around before the engine could be started. In each case fishermen in the boats had caught tuna from a school, and it was speculated that this may somehow have motivated the attacks.

photo E. Gould

SPHYRNA LEWINI
(Griffith & Smith, 1834)
MAO TUAMATA
SCALLOPED HAMMERHEAD SHARK[4]

Synonyms: Prior to the revision of this family in 1967[22], this species was known as *S. diplana*. Locally it was known as *matake* (Marquesas). Also, see *mao afata, S.* sp., synonyms.

Color: This species is a pale gray to brownish above fading to a yellowish, offwhite below The lower lobe of the tail and tips underneath the pectorals are black tipped, at least in younger specimens.

Morphology: See *mao afata, S.* sp., for comparative illustrations. The laterally expanded head has a curved forward margin (more so than *S. mokarran*) with a central notch and two lateral notches to each side of this central notch. The outermost lobe of the head, beyond the most lateral notch, projects forward, unlike *S. mokarran* which extends laterally or tapers backward. This results in a convex outline to the forward margin of the outermost lobe—lateral to the notch forward of the nasal pit. The apex of the first dorsal is about over the termination of the free dorsal base, and the forward margin of the first dorsal fin is about the same length as that of the forward margin of the lower lobe of the tail. This species is reported to reach 3 to 3.3 m (10 to 11ft), but most are about 2m (6 1/2ft).

Dentition: Teeth are reported as unserrated or slightly so in larger specimens and obliquely triangular with nearly stright outer margins.

Distribution: The scalloped hammer-

The scalloped hammerhead shark, sometimes aggressive, is only occasionally encountered due to it normal haunts at great depths.

photo D. Nelson

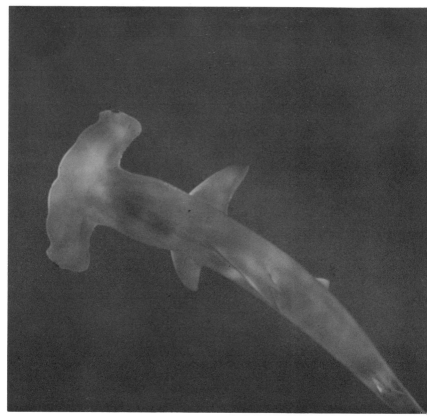

photo D. Nelson

head is known from all warm temperate and tropical oceans and is widely spread in water above 24°C (75°F).

Habitat: This species is basically pelagic and appears to frequent water in excess of 200 m (650ft)[15], although it is found at times near the surface.

Reproduction: The scalloped hammerhead appears to mature at just over 1.5 m (5ft) in the Western Atlantic and perhaps larger in the Pacific—in excess of 2 m (6 1/2ft). Pupping is spread throughout many months, but appears concentrated in spring (Northern Hemisphere). Pups appear to be born at a length of from 43 to 55 cm (17 to 22in). Larger females appear to produce litters with more pups ranging up to at least 30 and possibly more.

Activity: In Hawaii[15] adults move inshore for reproductive purposes. Pupping and apparently mating occur principally in Kaneohe Bay, Oahu. The smallest pups are concentrated in the turbid backwater of the bay. As these pups mature, they range into the central areas of the bay, where they form schools which move along the bottom, feeding predominantly at night. Eventually these pups depart apparently to live in dark pelagic depths. A similar pattern of behaviour may exist in Tahiti and certain Tua

154

Photo D. Nelson

notu Atolls where pups are found in turbid inshore waters.

Feeding: Although noted to feed on squid and octopus (cephalopods) and crab and shrimp (crustaceans), the scalloped hammerhead is basically a fish eater which feeds occasionally on other shark, including its own kind. It also shows a preference for rays, apparently being immune to the poisonous spines.

Disposition: The author found opportunity to dive under baited conditions with several individuals of this species in the Gulf Stream off Florida. They generally showed only passing interest in the divers, usually spending most of

Hammerhead sharks, like the scalloped hammerhead pictured, are generally identified by shape of the head (see p. 158-59).

the time at or around the bait. When the bait was removed, they remained in the area, often passing the divers. In one case, a new arrival closely circled two of the divers who were back to back to defend themselves, but realizing the divers weren't the source of the odor, it quickly assumed the general milling behavior of the others. This species is, however, implicated in attacks on man and should be respected, although in French Polynesia they are not regarded as particularly dangerous.

155

SPHYRNA MOKARRAN
(Rüppell, 1835)
TAMATAROA
GREAT HAMMERHEAD SHARK[4]

Synonyms: Prior to revision of the family[22], this species was known as *S. tudes*. Although a synonym for *S. mokarran*, *S. tudes* has remained a valid name for a hammerhead previously known as *S. bigelowei*. Also, see mao afata, *S.* sp., synonyms.

Color: This species is pale gray or beige above fading to a yellowish, off-white below.

Morphology: See *mao afata, S.* sp., for comparative illustrations. The laterally expanded head has a curved forward margin (but less so than *S. lewini*) with a central notch and two lateral notches to each side of the central notch. The outermost lobe of the head beyond the most lateral notch, just forward of the nasal pit, does not project forward as in *S. lewini* but extends laterally or tapers backward. This results in a concave outline to the forward margin of the outermost lobe—lateral to the notch forward of the nasal pit. The apex of the first dorsal is well behind the termination of the free rear tip of the same fin, and the forward margin of the first dorsal is notably longer than the forward margin of the lower lobe of the tail. This species is offically reported to reach 5.45 m (18ft) with some specimens estimated even longer. However most individuals are 4.58 m (15ft) or less.

Dentition: Teeth are reported as heavily serrated and obliquely triangular.

Distribution: The great hammerhead is wide spread in tropical waters, generally above 24°C (75°F). It is known in the Western Atlantic and the Eastern Pacific. The author's finding of this species in French Polynesia

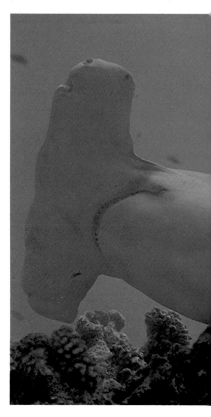

is the first report from Oceania[38].

Habitat: This species is more commonly found inshore than off, but it occurs commonly in either location. It is not infrequently found in and around atoll passes or lagoons.

Reproduction: Maturity is reached at over 3 m (10ft) with pupping occurring in late spring or summer (Northern Hemisphere). Pups number up to 38, again being more numerous with larger females, and they range from 56 to less than 70 cm (22 to 27in) long at birth.

Feeding: This species, although noted to eat crabs and squid, is also basically a fish eater, occasionally eating shark—including the flesh of its own kind.

156

It also expresses a preference for rays, apparently possessing immunity to the poison spines, as dozens have been found imbedded in the jaws and throat. The author has found that in French Polynesia this species appears especially fond of grouper, having caught one and attracted several individuals with such bait while never having had such results using shark or other bait.

Disposition: In French Polynesia this species is not considered aggressive toward man. In unbaited situations, it generally disregards divers and is seen only in passing. Under baited conditions, it may investigate divers near the stimulus source, but it will

Left: *The great hammerhead shark is identified by features of the head and the large falcate dorsal fin.* **Top**: *This nearly 15 ft (4.5 m), 1,500 lb (700 kg) specimen kept the author, his wife and associates entertained on three different occasions while diving in the same location on consecutive days.*

usually return to the source of the odor. Although encounters, close or otherwise, with these large sharks are a heart-stopping experience, native spearfishermen usually remain in the water. However, they only continue spearfishing after the shark has passed. In other parts of the world this species is a known attacker of man, and it should, because of its reputation elsewhere and its very large size, be regarded with great respect.

SPHYRNA SP.

(Potentially undescribed species)
MAO AFATA
SQUAREHEAD HAMMERHEAD
SHARK

Synonyms: Scientifically this species appears undescribed. Locally, those people who recognize the differences in hammerheads refer to this shark as *mao afata*. However, people, not recognizing the various species, apply this and the local names of other species, as well as the generalized name *mao hammera* of French/English origin, to any hammerhead.

Description: The following is based on local reports and the author's (30 sec.) observation of a specimen potentially of this description. It should be noted that the author was preoccupied in tagging this shark (tag failed to penetrate hide), and although noting differences, only later realized it fit the description of an apparently distinct species.

Color: The specimen noted by the author was a darker gray above than appears common to most hammerheads—possibly an individual variation not characteristic of the species.

Morphology: Regarding the local name, it translates literally as: *mao* = shark and *afata* = case or box, referring to the head, and this essentially sums up the description given locally. By comparison to the other species found locally; the scalloped hammerhead, *S. lewini*, and the great hammerhead, *S. mokarran*, the head of this possibly distinct species, although of similar lateral extension, is deeper giving the impression of a square rather than rectangular head. It does not fit the description of the bonnet head, *S. tiburo*, and similar sharks with more compressed or distinct shaped heads. The author's impression was a hammerhead with the above noted more

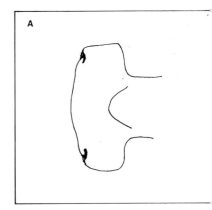

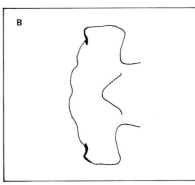

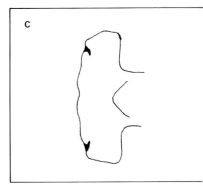

squarish shape to the head and smoother, strighter forward margi This particular shark was estimated just under 3 m (10ft).

Distribution: In inquiring about th

Diagramatic comparison of hammerhead species occuring in French Polynesia.

A. *Sphyrna media,* a species not thought to exceed 1.5 m (5 ft), of the inshore Tropical Eastern Pacific fauna most closely fits the description of mao afata. It is presented here not as representing the species but as a quide to the basic differences between local species.

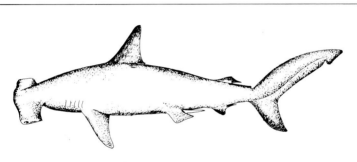

B. scalloped hammerhead shark, *Sphyrna lewini*

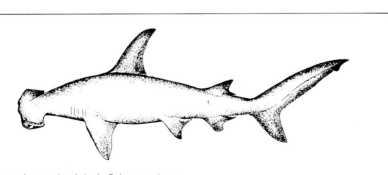

C. great hammerhead shark, *Sphyrna mokarran.*

pecies, the author has found local people throughout the Tuamotus, Windward and Leeward Society Islands and a person from the Gambier Island group who report that this species, as distinct from the others, occurs in the above areas. All agree that it is less common than the other species.

INDEX

* Indicates species in-depth discussion, including additional photos and suppli-mental information not otherwise in-dexed, e.g., color, morphology, distribu-tion, habitat, reproduction, feeding, disposition and related material.
⊖ Indicates identification in key.
⊘ Indicates global distribution on map.

A

C

California horn shark: (see *Heterodontus francisci*).

Cannibalism: 64; intrauterine, 20.

Carcharhinidae (requeim or gray shark family): 18, 96; ⊖ 89; ⊘ 92.

Carcharhinus albimarginatus (silvertip shark): 59; * 96-99; ⊖ 90; ⊘ 92.

C. altimus (bignose shark): ⊖ 90; ⊘ 92.

C. amblyrhynchos (gray reef shark): 18, 20, 44, 46, 48, 53-60, 64, 81, 111, 117; * 100-105; ⊖ 89; ⊘ 92: acoustic attraction in, 30-31; activity and movements, 42-43; display in, 53-58, 58, 60, 76, 78 - illustrated, 53, 56, 58 - toward other shark, 58; feeding - quantity and frequency, 28; longivity without food, 30; migrations, 46; packing behavior, 42; photos of, 19, 21, 31, 49, 54, 55, 59, 60-61, 65, 81; prey - normal size of, 46; respiration, 20.

C. falciformis (silky shark): 50; * 106-109; ⊖ 90; ⊘ 92; photo of, 51.

C. floridanus: 106 (see *C. falciformis*).

C. galapagensis (Galapagos shark): * 110-111; ⊖ 90; ⊘ 92; display, 59, 78; teeth, 24 - photo of, 25.

C. leucas (bull shark): * 112-113; ⊖ 89; ⊘ 92; fasting, 28; predation on other shark, 64; respiration, 20.

C. limbatus (blacktip shark): 122; * 114-117; ⊖ 90; ⊘ 92; activity, 44

C. longimanus (oceanic whitetip shark): * 118-121; ⊖ 90; ⊘ 92; fished, 12; reproduction, 18.

C. malpeloensis: 106 (see *C. falciformis*).

C. maou: 118 (see *C. longimanus*).

C. melanopterus (blackfin reef shark): 36, 47, 59, 64, 67, 75, 102, 117; * 122-125; ⊖ ⊘ 92; activity, 44; edibility, 12; photos of, 2, 47, 59, 66, 74-75; longivity without food, 30.

C. menisorrah: 100 (see *C. amblyrhynchos*).

C. nesiotes: 100 (see *C. amblyrhynchos*).

C. nicaraguensis: 112 (see *C. leucas*).

C. obscurus (dusky shark): 48, 90; ⊖ 90; ⊘ 92.

C. phorcys: 114 (see *C. limbatus*).

C. platyrhynchus: 96 (see *C. albimarginatus*).

C. pluembeus (sandbar shark): 12, 113; ⊖ 90; ⊘ 92.

C. springeri (Springer's reef shark): 20.

C. vanrooyeni: 112 (see *C. leucas*).

C. zambezensis: 112 (see *C. leucas*).

Carcharodon carcharias (white shark): 128; * 90; ⊖ 87; ⊘ 93; liver, 24; maneuverability and byouancy, 24; photo of, 91; porpoise - feeding on, 64; prey - size of, 46; reproduction, 18; record, 12, 90; swimming speed, 22.

C. megalodon (extinct white shark): 16.

Carpet, Nurse and Wobbegong shark family: (see Orectolobidae).

Cat shark family: (see Scyliorhinidae).

Caudal fin: 17.

Caudal keel: 17.

Centroscyllium granulosum (granular shark): ⊖ 88; ⊘ 93.

Cephaloscyllium ventriosum (swell shark): longivity without food, 30.

Ceratorichia: 13.

Cetorhinidae (basking shark family): ⊖ 87.

Cetorhinus maximus (basking shark): ⊖ 87; eggs, 18; fasting, 28; teeth, 26.

Chemical repellents: 69, 72.

Chimeras - rat fish (see Holocephalii).

Chlamydoselachidae (frill shark family): ⊖ 86.

Chondrichthyes (jawed cartilaginous fish - shark, rays and chimeras): 15, 85.

Chordata (endoskeletoned animals): 15, 85.

Cigar shark: (see *Isistius braziliensis*).

Ciguatera poisoning: 12.

Claspers: 17, 18 - photos of erect, 19.

Classification: 85.

CO_2 gas deterrents: 70.

Color perception: 41.

Commensalism: 62.

Common name derivations: 5.

Common thresher shark (see *Alopias vulpinus*).

Copulation: 16.

Courtship: 16, 36, 37.

Cone cells: 41.

Cupulae: defined, 36; diagramed, 33.

D

Dalatidae: ⊖ 89; ⊘ 92.

Deep water cat shark: (see *Apristurus spongiceps*).

Deification: of sharks, 8.

Dental formula: 17.

Denticles: 24; diagramed, 33.

Dentition: 24-28.

Deterrents: 68-72.

Display: (see Behavior).

Distant touch: 36.

Dogfish: (see *Squalus blainvillei* and *Scyliorhinus canicula*).

Dominance: (see Behavior - Dominance).

Dorsal fin: 17.

Drogues as deterrents: 70.

Dusky shark: (see *Carcharhinus obscurus*).

Dwarf shark: (see *Galeus piperatus*).

LITERATURE CITED

1. Arnoux, S. (personal communication).
2. Bagnis, R. (pers. comm.).
3. Bagnis, R., Mazellier, P., Bennett, J., and Christian, E. (1972). *Fishes of Polynesia*. Les éditions du pacifique, Papeete, Tahiti.
4. Bailey, R.M., Fitch, J.E., Herald, E.S., Lachner, E.A., Lindsey, C.C., Robins, R.C. and Scott, W.B. (1970). *A list of common and scientific names of fishes from the United States and Canada*. Sp. Pub. No. 6., Am. Fish. Soc., Washington, D.C.
5. Baldridge, D.H. (1972). *Accumulation and function of liver oil in Florida sharks.* Copeia, 2. pp. 306-325.
6. Baldridge, D.H. (1973). *Shark attack against man.* Tech. Rep. Off. Nav. Res. No. 104-148.
7. Baldridge, D.H. (1975). *Shark attack*. Berkely Medallion Books. N.Y.
8. Baldridge, D.H., and Williams, J. (1969). *Shark attack: feeding or fighting ?* Mil. Med. 34: 130-133.
9. Barlow, G.W. (1974). *Derivation of threat display in the gray reef shark*. Mar. Behav. Physiol. 3: pp. 71-81.

10. Bass, A.J., D'Aubrey, J.D., and Kistnasamy (1973). *Sharks of the East coast of Southern Africa. I. The genus* Carcharhinus *(Carcharhinidae).* S. Afr. Ass. Mar. Biol. Res., Oceanogr. Res. Inst., Invest. Rept. No. 33 pp. 1-168.

11. Boyd, E. (1975). *Monster teeth of Chesapeake Bay.* Skindiver Mag. (January).

12. Brown, T.W. (1973). *Sharks: the search for a repellent.* Angus and Robertson, Sydney.

13. Clark, E. (1975). *Into the lairs of "sleeping" sharks.* Nat. Geo. Mag., April pp. 570-584.

14. Clark, E., and von Schmidt, K. (1965). *Sharks of the central Gulf Coast of Florida.* Bull. Mar. Sci. 15: I pp. 13-83.

15. Clarke, T.A. (1971). *The ecology of the scalloped hammerhead shark,* Sphyrna lewini, *in Hawaii.* Pac. Sci. 25 (2) pp. 133-144.

16. Cousteau, J.Y., and Cousteau, P.C. (1970). *The shark: splendid savage* of the sea. Doubleday & Co., Inc. N.Y.

17. Compagno, L.J.V. (1976). *Illustrated key to orders and families of living sharks.* January 20 printing. Dept. of Bio. Sci., Stanford Univ., Stanford, Calif. 94305.

18. Cropp, B. (1964). *Shark Hunters.* Rigby Ltd., Adelaide.

19. Davies, D.H., Lochner, J.D.A., and Smith, E.D. (1963). *Preliminary investigations on the hearing of sharks.* Oceanog. Res. Inst. (South Africa) Invest. Rept. No. 7, 10 pp.

20. Frankbonner (pers. comm.)

21. Garrick, J.A.F. (1967). *Revision of sharks of genus Isurus with description of a new species (galeoidea, Lamnidae).* Proc. of the U.S. Nat. Museum. 118: 3537 pp. 663-694.

22. Gilbert, C. (1967). *A revision of the hammerhead sharks (family Sphyrnidae).* Pro. of the U.S. Nat. Museum. 119: 3539 p. 88.

23. Gilbert, P.W. (1962). *The behavior of sharks.* Sci. Am., July.

24. Gilbert, P.W. (1963). *The visual apparatus of sharks.* In Sharks and Survival. P.W. Gilbert (éd.). D.C. Heath Co., Boston.

25. Gilbert, P.W. (1968). *The shark: barbarian and benefactor.* Bio. Sci. 18: 2 pp. 946-950.

26. Gilbert, P.W., and Gilbert, D. (1973). *Sharks and shark deterrents.* Underwater Jour. 5: 2 No. 2 pp. 69-78.

27. Gilbert, P.W., and Heath, G.W. (1972). *The clasper siphon sac mechanism in* Squalus acanthias *and* Mustelus canis. Compt. Biochem. Physiol. 2: 42A, pp. 97 119.

28. Gilbert, P.W., Irvine, B., and Martini, F.H. (1971). *Shark porpoise behavioral interactions.* Amer. Zool. 11: 4 Nov. p. 80.

29. Hickman, C.P. (1961). *Integrated principles of zoology.* C.V. Mosby Co., St Louis.

30. Hobson, E.S. (1963). *Feeding behavior in three species of shark.* Pac. Sci. 17: 2.

31. Hubbs, C.L. (1945). *Occurrence of the bramble shark in Calif.* Calif. Fish and Game. 31: 2 pp. 64-67.

32. Jensen, R. (pers. comm.)

33. Johnson, R.H. (unpublished data).

34. Johnson, R.H., and Nelson, D.R. (1973). *Agonistic display in the gray reef shark,* Carcharhinus menisorrah, *and its relationship to attacks on man.* Copeia 1: pp. 76-84.

35. Johnson, R.H., and Nelson, D.R. (In press). *Copulation and possible odor (olfaction) mediated pair formation in two species of* Carcharhinid *sharks.*

36. Johnson, R.H., and Nelson, D.R. (in preparation. *An agonistic attack, and factors affecting same, by the gray reef shark,* Carcharhinus amblyrhynchos.

37. Johnson, R.H., and Nelson, D.R. (in prep.). *Behavior of the gray reef shark,* Carcharhinus amblyrhynchos, *including telemetric and conventional tagging studies of movement (daily and long term) and social behavior.*

38. Johnson, R.H., and Nelson, D.R. (in prep.). *Sharks of French Polynesia.*

39. Johnson, R.H., and Nelson, D.R. (unpub. data).

40. Kalmijn, A.J. (1971). *The electric sense of sharks and rays.* J. Exp.

Biol. 55: pp. 371-383.

41. Kato, S., Springer, S., and Wagner M.H. (1967). *Field guide to Eastern Pacific and Hawaiian sharks*. U.S. Dep. Interior, Fish and Wildl. Serv. Circular 271 p. 47.

42. Klimley, P.L. (pers. comm.).

43. Lagler, K.F., Bardach, J.E., and Miller, R.R. (1962). *Ichthyology*. John Wiley & Sons, Inc. N.Y.

44. Linneaweaver, T.H. III, and Backus, H. (1970). *The natural history of sharks*. The Trinity Press, London.

45. McNair, R. (1975). *Sharks I have known*. Skindiver Mag. (January).

46. McNair, R. (pers. comm.).

47. McWhirther, N., and McWirther, R. (1975). *Guiness book of world records*. Bantam Books, Inc. N.Y.

48. Myrberg, A.A. (1974). *The behavior of the bonnethead shark*, Sphyrna tiburo. Copeia 2: pp. 358-374.

49. Myrberg, A.A. (pers. comm.).

50. Neal, J. (pers. comm.).

51. Nelson, D.R. (unpub. data).

52. Nelson, D.R., and Gruber, D.R. (1963). *Sharks: attraction to low-frequency sounds*. Sciences. 142: 3594, pp. 975-977.

53. Nelson, D.R., and Johnson, R.H. (1972). *Acoustic attractions of Pacific reef sharks: effects of pulse intermittancy and variability*. Comp. Biochem. Physiol., 42A: pp. 85-95.

54. Nelson, D.R., and Johnson, R.H. (in prep.). *Behavior of the reef whitetip*, Triaenodon obesus, *at Rangiroa Atoll, French Polynesia*.

55. Nelson, D.R., and Johnson, R.H. (unpub. data).

56. Parker, G.H. (1914). *The directional influence of the sense of smell in dogfish*. Bull. U.S. Bur. Fisheries 33: pp. 61-68.

57. Randall, J.E. (1961). *Let a sleeping shark lie*. Sea Frontiers 7: 3 pp. 153-159.

58. Randall, J.E. (1963). *Dangerous sharks of the Western Atlantic*. In *Sharks and Survival*. P.W. Gilbert (ed.). D.C. Heath and Co., Boston.

59. Randall, J.E. (pers. comm.).

60. Randall, J.E., and Helfman, G.S. (1973). *Attacks on humans by the blacktip reef shark*, Carcharhinus melanopterus. Pac. Sci. 27: 3 pp. 226-238.

61. Romer, A.S. (1970). *The vertebrate body*. W.E. Saunders Co., London.

62. Schaffer, B. (1967). *Comments on elasmobranch evolution*. In *Sharks, Skates and Rays*. P.W. Gilbert, R.G. Mathewson, and D.P. Rall (eds). The John Hopkins Press. Baltimore.

63. Sciarotta, T. (1974). *A telemetric study of the blue shark*. Prionace glauca, *near Santa Catalina Island, Calif*. Masters Thesis. Calif. State Univ., Long Beach.

64. Tapu, J. (pers. comm.).

65. Tester, A.L. (1963). *Olfaction, gustation and the common chemical sense in sharks*. In *Sharks and Survival*. P.W. Gilbert (ed). D.C. Heath and Co., Boston.

66. Tester, A.L. (1963). *The role of olfaction in shark predation*. Pac. Sci. 22: 2 pp. 145-170.

67. Tester, A.L. (1969). *Cooperative shark research control program. Final report for 1967-69*. Univ. of Hawaii, Honolulu.

68. Tester, A.L., and Kato, S. (1966). *Visual target descrimination in blacktip sharks*, Carcharhinus melanopterus, *and gray sharks*. C. menisorrah. Pac. Sci. 20: 4 pp. 461-471.

69. Thorson, T.B. (1971). *Movements of bull sharks*, Carcharhinus leucas. *between the Caribbean Sea and Lake Nicaragua demonstrated by tagging*. Copeia 2: pp. 336-338.

70. Tokoragi, C. (pers. comm.). *Translations of interviews with local inhabitants of Rangiroa Atoll, French Polynesia*.

71. Wass, R.C. (1971). *A comparative study of the life history, distribution and ecology of the sandbar shark and the gray reef shark*. PhD Thesis. Univ. of Hawaii, Honolulu.

72. Williams, T. (pers. comm.). *Taped conversations on sharks of the Cook Islands*.

73. Wood, F.G., Caldwell, D.K., and Caldwell, M.C. (1970). *Behavioral interactions between porpoises and sharks*. In *Investigations on Cetacea*. B. Pilleri (ed) 2: pp. 264-277.

74. Young, W.E. *Shark shark ! thirty years of shark hunting*. Hurst & Blackett Ltd., London.

photo C. Johnson

about the author

RICHARD HANSLEE JOHNSON, the oldest of three sons, was born a citizen of the U.S. on October 8, 1940 to parents of German ancestry. After spending three years in the U.S. Navy, he entered college and majored in biology. As a graduate of California State Polytechnic University, Pomona (Bachelor of Science degree) and California State University, Long Beach (Master of Arts degree), he ultimately specialized in Ichthyology and Animal Behavior concentrating on investigations of sharks. His master's thesis was a comparative behavioral study of two species of sharks common to the California coast. He began doctoral studies at the University of California, Los Angeles which were interrupted by shark research expeditions, ultimately taking him to the South Pacific where he met his French wife, Chantal. During these years he pioneered significant research concerning shark attack behavior including senior authorship of the first scientific papers[34][36] to conclusively provide direct evidence indicating a second "non-feeding" motivation for attacks on man. Over the years, in the quest for knowledge about sharks, Mr. Johnson has visited many remote regions of the world on projects sponsored by various agencies including the Office of Naval Research, National Geographic Society and the Atomic Energy Commission. He is presently the Executive Director of S.E.A. Institute, Inc., 2018 Pacific Ave., Long Beach, California 90806, an organization concentrating on various aspects of shark research.

acknowledgements

The author wishes to extend his sincerest appreciation to Dr. Donald R. Nelson of California State University, Long Beach with whom he has worked for many years studying shark behavior. Some of the experiences and new information provided in this book have resulted from the author's association with his research program supported by the U.S. Office of Naval Research and the National Geographic Society. Additional information has been obtained during research supported by S.E.A. Institute, Inc. as a result of the author's independent shark research project. The author, on behalf of S.E.A. Institute, Inc., is grateful to the many businesses which have helped support research, notably: Avon Inflatable Craft, Electro Oceanics, Evinrude Outboard Motors, Healthways and Peter Storm Limited. Gratitude is also extended to Drs, Jack Garrick, Perry Gilbert and Leighton Taylor, for their assistance in preparing this publication, and the numerous other persons, who have helped make this book possible, including the many who assisted expedition research. Among these people special mention is due Mr. Terry Sciarotta, who constructed many of the telemetry tags used on expedition research and Mr. James McKibben, whose long and competent assistance was valuable Moreover, appreciation is extended to the governments of the Cook Islands and French Polynesia, especially Messrs. Sixte Stein, Celestin Tokoragi, Jean Tapu and Mr. Philippe Siu of Service de la Pêche, Mr. Jean de Chazeaux of C.N.E.X.O. and Mr. Marc Darnois of Relations et Echanges Culturels, for their cooperation in assisting shark investigations in French Polynesian water. Last but not least, the author is most grateful to those who have contributed supplimental photographic material.

Lay out by J.-L. Saquet
Studio Les Editions du Pacifique
Drawings after: p 32—33 A & B, 38 B & 40 — Gilbert 23;
p 32 B — Davies et. al. 19; p 37 — Johnson & Nelson 35; p 53, 56 & 58
Johnson & Nelson 34; p 86—89 Compagno 17
(also p 158 & 159) Kato et. al. 41.

Nature Series
Scientific editor: Bernard Salvat

Publisher's Number: 246
November 1991
Printed in Singapore